Excel 2023

The Ultimate Guide to Master Microsoft Excel | Learn How to Use Simple and Powerful Formulas, Pivot Tables, Charts, and Much More with Step-by-Step Instruction in Less than 7 min a Day

By

BERNARD WOOLRIDGE

Owen County Public Library
10 South Montgomery Street
Spencer, IN 47460
812-829-3392

© **Copyright 2023 by BERNARD WOOLRIDGE - All rights reserved.**

This document is geared towards providing exact and reliable information in regards to the topic and issue covered. The publication is sold with the idea that the publisher is not required to render accounting, officially permitted, or otherwise, qualified services. If advice is necessary, legal or professional, a practiced individual in the profession should be ordered.

- From a Declaration of Principles which was accepted and approved equally by a Committee of the American Bar Association and a Committee of Publishers and Associations.

In no way is it legal to reproduce, duplicate, or transmit any part of this document in either electronic means or in printed format. Recording of this publication is strictly prohibited, and any storage of this document is not allowed unless with written permission from the publisher. All rights reserved.

The information provided herein is stated to be truthful and consistent, in that any liability, in terms of inattention or otherwise, by any usage or abuse of any policies, processes, or directions contained within is the solitary and utter responsibility of the recipient reader. Under no circumstances will any legal responsibility or blame be held against the publisher for any reparation, damages, or monetary loss due to the information herein, either directly or indirectly.

Respective authors own all copyrights not held by the publisher.

The information herein is offered for informational purposes solely and is universal as so. The presentation of the information is without a contract or any type of guarantee assurance.

The trademarks that are used are without any consent, and the publication of the trademark is without permission or backing by the trademark owner. All trademarks and brands within this book are for clarifying purposes only and are owned by the owners themselves, not affiliated with this document.

Table of Contents

Introduction 7

Chapter 1: Elements of Microsoft Excel 9

   1.1 What is Microsoft Excel, and how does it work? 9

   1.2 How to work with excel? 13

   1.3 Excel menu 17

   1.4 Minimal Hierarchy 17

   1.5 Editing Data 20

   1.6 Preview Option 20

   1.7 Data Entry 21

   1.8 Selection Zone 26

   1.9 Handling of Workbooks and Worksheets 28

Chapter 2: Editing in Excel 34

   2.1 Edit the contents of the cells 35

   2.2 Cells, rows, and columns can be cleared or deleted 35

   2.3 Remove any cell's contents, formats, or comments 36

   2.4 Undo & Redo Mistakes 36

   2.5 Separate text in different cells 36

   2.6 Replace or find data 37

   2.7 Text and numbers can be found and replaced 38

   2.8 Make use of a filtering editing technique 38

   2.9 Display a subset of rows in a list by using filters 39

   2.10 You can use wildcard characters to find text or numbers 40

   2.11 Make columns out of copied text data 40

Chapter 3: Working with Charts 42

3.1 Why Charts are used? 43
3.2 The fundamental idea 43
3.3 Elements of a Chart 44
3.4 Various Type of Charts 45
3.5 Creating a Chart 49
3.6 Create a Chart in one step 49
3.7 Make a chart out of non-adjacent selections 49
3.8 Select a different chart type 50
3.9 Saving & Retrieval of Charts...51

Chapter 4: Advanced Data Retrieval 52
4.1 Pivot Table..52
4.2 Creation of a pivot table report....................................59
4.3 Deletion of a Pivot Table report 63
4.4 QUERY: A Reliable inquiry counter 66
4.5 How to Retrieve Data 69

Chapter 5: Functions 71
5.1 Date & Time Functions.. 71
5.2 Information Functions...78
5.3 Logical Functions 84
5.4 Lookup & Reference Functions 96

Chapter 6: Shortcut Keys in Excel 115
6.1 Moving and scrolling in a worksheet or workbook.... 116
6.2 Keys for previewing and printing a document 118
6.3 Key for working with worksheets, charts, and macros
.... 119
6.4 Keys for use with Pivot Table and PivotChart reports.
.... 121

6.5 First and Fast Tip *122*

Conclusion **123**

Introduction

Microsoft Excel is a spreadsheet programme that may be used to store and analyse numerical and statistical data. Microsoft Excel includes a number of tools for doing various tasks, including computations, graphing tools, pivot tables, macro programming, and so on. It works with Mac OS X, Windows, Android, and iOS, among other operating systems.

A table made up of columns and rows is what an Excel spreadsheet is. Columns are typically assigned alphabetical letters, whereas rows are typically assigned numbers. A cell is the intersection of two columns or rows. The letter that represents a column and the number that represents a row make up a cell's address. Excel is a spreadsheet program developed by Microsoft.

People who handle accounts and some aspects of financial professions that require forecasting features with a combination of built-in capabilities can utilize this package as a very clever tool for their personal domestic/enterprise-level work performance, and they are fully qualified to use Excel. As you may know, Excel is a component of Microsoft Office and is dedicated to calculation, analysis, charting, and other spreadsheet solutions. It is also known as ESS, and it was previously used with packages such as LOTUS-123, VP Planner, VisiCalc, SUPER CALC, Quattro Pro, and other spreadsheet solutions.

The concept of a spreadsheet is similar in all packages, but the presentation and performance of each package differ significantly, with Excel being the most advanced spreadsheet solution available today. Excel 2021 is a spreadsheet tool that allows you to swiftly and precisely interact with data. Many of the functions are the same as in prior Excel versions. It includes various tools for organizing and changing data, as well as charts for showing data and much more. Let's say you'd want to brush up on your Excel skills or have never used it before. In such a case, this book will show you how to work with rows, columns, data formatting, basic formulae, and functions in spreadsheet software. You'll notice a few new features in Excel 2021. Among other things, you'll learn about the text, numeric, and logical functions.

Chapter 1: Elements of Microsoft Excel

1.1 What is Microsoft Excel, and how does it work?

The most widely used spreadsheet program is Microsoft Excel. Although all of Microsoft Excel's numerous features and capabilities can be frightening, the interface is intuitive and easy to use. However, you can quickly learn the fundamentals of Excel, and after you've done so, learning the more advanced features of the application is rather simple. Excel isn't just a spreadsheet tool; it's also an application development environment with data analysis and display capabilities that go beyond those of a normal spreadsheet. This implies that, because of Excel's features, you may design a comprehensive, personalized application that performs exactly what you need.

- References in dialog boxes collapse the dialog box to a smaller size.

- Easier entry of range dialog boxes that accept range references.

- The new IntelliMouse pointing device uses the wheel button to scroll or zoom.

- Drag the boundary of a range of cells to move the range to another workbook or worksheet window for better drag-and-drop editing.

- Save a list of workbooks as in previous versions.
- Multiple Undo up to the last 16 actions.
- Yes, to All option when you quit with multiple files open which you can choose to save all the files before exiting.
- Closing multiple files.
- As you move the highlight for the active cell, the row and column titles will change.
- The full-Screen command is to view more worksheets.
- The File Menu's Save Workspace option preserves a list of open workbooks, their sizes, and their placements so that the screen appears the same the next time you access the workspace file.

All of the mentioned alternatives are entirely compatible with all users and all available applications to do the same task. However, some Excel functions have been created in such a way that users can attain them. The following characteristics include:

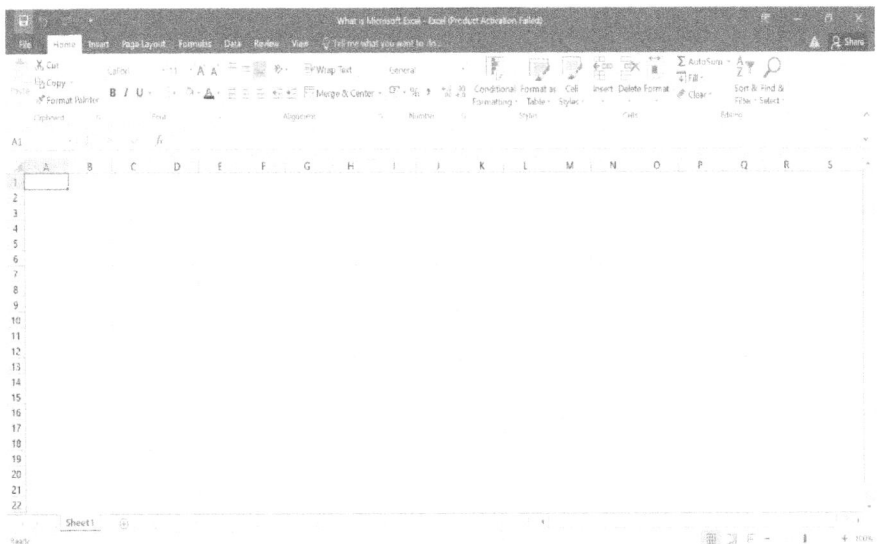

- **Calculation and examination:** This software's calculation and analysis features are so beneficial in practice that anyone can perform the assignment with ease, whether using universal fixed data or fluctuating data. For example, numerous sheets will hold all of the data connected to each cell or sheet, so altering the data in one cell or sheet will update the entire formulation, displaying the complete dependent result.

- **Charting**: Excel's charting function allows you to create charts with the least amount of effort and with the most compatible features. The charts created by Excel are fully integrated or non-embedded, allowing for the process of altering layouts, orientations, and other types of flexibility to be completed automatically.

- **Auto formatting with built-in functions:** Data formatting can also be automated using built-in functions. Users do not need to worry about the one-line procedure or other elements in this case. In fact, the entire portion is designed to assist the user.

- **Advanced query features:** As you may know, the most basic piece of any worksheet is the cell, which includes all of the information in the form of rows/columns or sheets, where query features allow you to search for records quickly based on the criteria you provide.

- **The interface between Office components and web-based data is the quickest and easiest**: Because the in-built HTML editor conducts the entire job for all users, the latest function of Excel allows you to finish the operation and link the documents with each other depending on any topic through intranet and internet. You can add any document as a sub-info of any site directly.

- **Data processing on a large scale**: Assume that your company has four branches and that in order to collect the daily production report, your database, which is in the form of worksheets and workbooks, must be connected, and the current production status must be collected. Such a task can be completed quickly and effectively by using the advanced features of Excel.

- **Other Excel Features:** Excel has a variety of other features that enhance its functionality.
- **Specification:** Excel makes it simple to complete the following activities.

➢ Analysis

➢ Forecasting

➢ Financial solutions

➢ Charting

➢ Complex lookup tables

➢ On-line data manipulation

➢ Data on the Web

➢ The interface of data with other office families as well as other software

Apart from this, a user can explore a variety of choices while working with Excel to do practical tasks. Let's start with the basics of Excel before moving on to more advanced topics.

1.2 How to work with excel?

If a new user wishes to get started with Excel, it is strongly recommended that they do it in a methodical manner. If you're serious about becoming a skilled Excel user, remember to follow the stages below. Once you've completed these steps, you'll have a much better understanding of Excel's conceptual aspects. The steps are as follows:

- Begin the Excel Worksheet Session
- Using single or many sheets
- Calculation
- Saving
- Worksheet Editing and Formatting
- Graphical representation
- Advanced characteristics
- Excel apps that may be accessed via the web

For conceptual clarity, a brief description of each stage is provided.

a) **Start the session:** After opening an Excel session, it displays a set of worksheets with three family members, multiple rows/columns, and cells as previously discussed, and it is ready to address all data manipulation issues. You can begin entering data at this point. Adding alternative fonts, colors, scaling size, relating data with the proper formula, and so forth. Some of the tasks will be completed automatically, while the remaining must be completed according to your specifications.

b) **Using Single and Multiple Sheets:** All of the aforementioned data will be entered into cells, which are a part of the worksheet where you have the option of working with single or multiple sheets. If a financial or annual presentation involves summary data on the main page and associated data on a different area of the same worksheet or on a new worksheet, the user can organize the data as they see fit if a user wishes to accomplish all of the needed tasks on the same worksheet or on numerous sheets. The main data will be calculated and linked to the presentation's main page, where you will have the option of completing the task through basic data linking and hyperlinking to leap inside the document upon the user's request. Multiple sheets can be utilized to maintain all of the data separated into pieces that can subsequently be linked.

c) **Calculation:** Based on the data segments, the calculation will be performed after the final compilation of the full statement using Formulae & Functions (which are divided into different categories). There are numerous built-in functions and equations.

d) **Saving:** It is essential that you save the input data for future access because it is required to save the working status after entering the data and doing calculations. It offers a few options, which we'll go through later.

e) **Editing & Formatting Worksheets:** Users need to be able to edit and format worksheets in order to manipulate and rectify errors. Spelling corrections, data re-entry, and other such things are examples of editing. Changing the layout of any data in a worksheet is referred to as formatting.

f) **Graphical Demonstration:** To make the data display more comprehensible, the entered data will be translated into a graphical format. It would be much easier for you to accomplish the assignment with a decent concept if you are familiar with various types of graphs.

g) **Advanced characteristics:** The advanced features include Pivot tables and other unique capabilities that can be utilized to present entire professional reports.

h) **Data Interaction with Other Office Family Members:** The data entered can be modified in various formats using other packages on the same platform or on distinct platforms. Excel data, for example, can be converted, connected, and hyperlinked with Word, PowerPoint, and Access.

i) **Excel web-based applications:** The web player or new web spectator can take advantage of the web-based applications' significant potential, such as submitting data for the same on the web online/offline. After taking a quick glance at the menus available in Excel, you should be able to complete the task quickly. We'll talk about the menus available in Excel in the next step; it contains a lot of the same menu options as Word, but the different alternatives are explained here.

1.3 Excel's menu

The menu is essentially identical in all of the office family components; however, due to the nature of the software, it differs slightly. After you've gone through all of the menus, you'll see the following common menu, which has nearly identical options, but the main difference between the sub-pad and new pad is listed below. With extra menus available, it is much easier for anyone to finish the work after using the typical menus and their possibilities. Each menu's specifics will be detailed later.

The easiest way to learn

Before you begin your Excel session, you should familiarize yourself with the basics of the program. Because Excel is included with all of Office 2000's components, you won't go over the common functions available with it. The four learning series have been provided here for the convenience of users; please go through the minimal hierarchical series.

1.4 Minimal Hierarchy

If you're new to Excel, you should be familiar with its basic hierarchy. In fact, this is where the basic functional unit begins:

Cell

Any spreadsheet solution's basic working unit is the cell. This package's cell is where all of the entries/data entry takes place. Each cell's address is determined by the Column and Row, i.e., A5, CH255, where A and CH are column addresses and 5 and 255 are row addresses. In Excel, each cell may hold up to 32000 characters.

Row/Column

The entire worksheet is organized into rows and columns, each of which can hold one or more records. To further comprehend this, consider a register, which is divided into rows and columns and is analogous to the notion of ROWS/COLUMN/CELL, in which a sheet is divided into rows and a columnar arrangement of horizontal and vertical lines with a Cell junction. Excel has a total of 65536 rows and 256 columns, which are divided into cells by default (Total cells - 65536 x 256, Total data that may be entered - 65536 x 256 x 32000 characters).

Worksheet

A worksheet is like a separate sheet of any record that is divided into a large number of horizontal and vertical lines (rows and columns) with Cell crossings. A sheet linked to a book or register can be presumed to be a standard worksheet. By default, there will be three worksheets available, which can be raised or lowered depending on the needs of the user.

Workbook The concept of a workbook, which is a standard collection of worksheets in Excel, is now easier to grasp. If you want to create a good salary analysis model in Excel, you can enter all of the wage information for January in Sheet 1, February in Sheet 2, and March in Sheet 3. After the calculations, the fourth sheet can be used to offer a complete analytical presentation of the quarterly report, with the option to skip the unneeded calculations for making differences (which will automatically generate the final report) and final answers.

Excel File

The workbook in Excel is referred to as an XLS file or an MS-Excel file. This type of file can be connected or transferred into a variety of forms, including text, database, cell-based data input, and so on, making it more useful for all users who want to work with data in a meaningful way. The above-mentioned hierarchy explains the principle and dependability of each Excel element. Data can be typed into cells, and calculations can be performed according to the user's needs. For example, if the total salary is calculated using BASIC, DA, TA, and HRA, all related data will be entered in the cell, and one specific cell will contain the salary calculation formula, and the result can be presented as a normal data model or a complete graphical presentation of the salary model using the charting facility. When each step is done according to the task, the user should store it for later use, such as previewing or printing the existing data model. If you're a web player, you can save the same data model in HTML format and publish it as a URL.

1.5 Editing Data

The entire working methodology of worksheet and workbook handling revolves around the above-mentioned phases, i.e., if an error is detected after data entering, it will be corrected using editing tools, which may include fairly common tools like cut/copy/paste, etc. When all of the prerequisites are met, you will be able to see a preview of the data.

1.6 Preview Option

This series describes a hypothetical method of data handling in Excel, such as after data entry, it can be manipulated using the many tools available for manipulation, and after the task is completed, a Preview will present a clear picture of the existing data, and in the case of graphical presentation, it can be presented in the same manner using the charting facility. Charting, goal-seek, and pivot tables are examples of tools that aid in the analysis and, ultimately, linking to more than a cell/sheet or a workbook utilizing linking strategies. Many more elements are also accessible for the users' convenience to finish the task, which can be provided in a hierarchical series of data representations. The following part is specifically created to provide you with comprehensive Excel knowledge.

1.7 Data Entry

Enter data in cells/worksheet

i. **Enter numbers, text, a date, or a time**

   a) Select the cell into which you wish to enter data.

   b) Press ENTER or TAB after typing the date. To separate the portions of a date, use a slash or a hyphen. As an example, type 15/10/2021 or 15th-Oct-2021. Type a space and then an or pm after the time to enter a time based on the 12-hour clock. For instance, at 9:00 p.m. Microsoft Excel, on the other hand, enters the time as AM.

ii. **Using a formula:**

   a) Select the cell where the formula should be entered.

   b) Enter = (an equal sign). Microsoft Excel inserts an equal sign for you when you select Edit Formula or Paste Function.

   c) Fill in the formula.

   d) Press the ENTER key.

iii. **Fill in the same information in multiple cells at the same time:**

a) Choose the cells into which you want to enter data. The cells can be next to each other or not.

b) Enter the data and press CTRL+ENTER.

iv. **Using several worksheets to enter or modify the same data**: Changes you make to a selection on the active sheet are applied in the corresponding cells on all other selected sheets when you select a group of sheets. The data on the other sheets might be changed.

a) Choose the worksheets where you'll be entering data.

b) Choose the cell or range of cells into which you want to enter data.

c) In the first selected cell, type or edit the data.

d) TAB or ENTER to return to the previous screen.

e) Click any unselected sheet to cancel a selection of several sheets.

Click any unselected sheet to cancel a selection of several sheets. If no unselected sheets are shown, right-click a selected sheet's tab and choose Ungroup Sheets from the shortcut menu.

v. **Fill in repeated entries in a column quickly:** Microsoft Excel fills in the remaining characters for you if the first few characters you write in a cell match an existing record in that column. Solely entries containing text or a combination of text and numbers are finished by Microsoft Excel; entries containing only numbers, dates, or times are not completed.

Press ENTER to accept the suggested entry. The completed entry follows the same uppercase and lowercase letter pattern as the previous entries. Continue typing if you want to replace the automatically entered characters. BACKSPACE can be used to erase the automatically typed characters.

vi. **Enter numbers, text, a date, or a time:**

a) Select the cell into which you want to enter information.

b) Press ENTER or TAB after typing the date.

To separate the portions of a date, use a slash or a hyphen; for example, type 15/10/2021 or 15-Oct-2021.

Type a space and then a.m. or p.m. after the time to enter a time based on the 12-hour clock; for example, 9:00 p.m. Otherwise, the time is entered as AM in Microsoft Excel.

vii. **Hide a column or a row:** Choose the rows or columns you'd want to hide. Point to either Row or Column in the Format menu, then click Hide.

viii. Demonstrate concealed rows and columns:

a) Select cells in the row above and below the concealed rows to reveal the hidden rows. Select cells in the column to the left and

b) the column to the right of the concealed columns to reveal them.

c) Point to either Row or Column on the Format menu, then click Unhide.

ix. Text, cells, ranges, rows, and columns can all be selected:

To Select	Do this
Text in a cell	Text in a cell Select the cell, double-click in it, and then select the text in the cell if cell editing is enabled. If cell editing is disabled, select the cell and then the text in the formula bar.
A single cell	To move to the cell, click it and use the arrow keys.
A range of cells	Drag from the first cell in the range to the last cell in the range.
All cells on a worksheet	Select all by pressing the Select All button.

Cell ranges or non-adjacent cells	After selecting the first cell or range of cells, hold CTRL and select the remaining cells or ranges.
A wide variety of cells	Hold down SHIFT and click the first cell in the range, then click the last cell in the range. You can scroll down to see the last cell.
An entire row	Select the row heading by clicking it.
Adjacent columns or rows	Drag across the row or column headings. Or select the first column or row; then hold down SHIFT and select the last column or row.
Nonadjacent rows or columns	Select the first row or column, and then hold down CTRL and select the other rows or columns.
More or fewer cells than the active selection	Click the last cell you want to include in the new selection while holding down SHIFT. The new selection is the rectangular range between the active cell and the cell you click.

x. **Numbers, dates, and times aren't displayed as expected:**

a) The number format used to the cells in Microsoft Excel determines how numbers, dates, and times are shown on a worksheet. Select the cells to modify the number format. Click Cells on the Format menu, then the Number tab, then the category and format you wish. Click the cell and press CTRL+SHIFT+# to use the default date format. In place of a number, press CTRL+SHIFT+@ #### to use the default time format. When a cell has a number, date, or time that is broader than the cell or a date or time formula that returns a negative result, the cell receives a #### error value. Increase the column's width if necessary.

b) Regional settings: The default format for money, dates, hours, and numbers is determined by the options you choose in Control Panel's Regional Settings.

1.8 Selection Zone

i.   Select blank cells

a) Choose a range that contains the cells you want to select. Click any cell on the active worksheet to select all cells of this kind.

b) Select GoTo from the Edit menu.

c) Click Special.

d) Click Blanks.

ii. Select cells that contain comments:

a) Select the range that includes the type of cells you want to select. To select all cells of this type on the active worksheet, click any cell.

b) Select GoTo from the Edit menu.

c) Click Special.

d) Click Blanks.

iii. Select cells that contain formulas:

a) Choose a range that contains the cells you want to pick. Click any cell on the active worksheet to select all cells of this kind.

b) Select Go To from the Edit menu.

c) Click Special.

d) Select the check box next to the type of data you want to select by clicking Formulas.

iv. Select between named ranges and cell references:

To select	Do this
A cell range with a name	Select the range in the Name box.
Two or more named ranges	Select the first range in the Name box, then hold CTRL and select the other ranges.

| Specific cells not in a named range Select Edit GoTo. | In the Reference box, type the cell reference for the cell or range of cells. |

v.   Only visible cells should be chosen:

This approach is used to choose a range that crosses hidden rows or columns but does not include hidden cells.

a) Choose a range.

b) Select GoTo from the Edit menu.

c) Select Special.

d) Only visible cells are selected.

vi.   Cancel a selection of cells:

Click any cell on the worksheet to cancel a selection of cells.

1.9 Handling of Workbooks and Worksheets

i.   Considering workbooks and worksheets

a) **Workbooks:** It is a file in which you work and save your data in Microsoft Excel. You can organize many types of relevant information in a single file because each workbook can contain many sheets.

b) **Worksheets:** Worksheets can be used to list and examine data. You can simultaneously enter and update data on numerous worksheets, as well as execute calculations using data from many worksheets. When you make a chart, you have the option of putting it on the worksheet with its data or on a separate chart sheet.

c) **Sheet tabs:** The sheets' names are listed on tabs at the bottom of the workbook window. Click the sheet tabs to navigate from one sheet to the next.

ii. **About Navigate through a worksheet by moving your cursor over it:** Click any cell on a worksheet to navigate between cells, or use the arrow keys. When you move to a cell, that cell becomes active. Use the scroll bars to see a different part of the sheet.

To Navigate	Do This
Up or down one row	Use the arrows in the vertical scroll bar to move up and down.
Left or right one column	Toggle the horizontal scrollbar with the arrows.
Up or down one window	In the vertical scroll, click above or below the scroll box.
Left or right one window	In the horizontal scroll bar, click to the left or right of the scroll box.
A significant distance drag	Scroll to the approximate relative position in the scroll box. Hold down SHIFT when dragging on a large worksheet.

iii. **Change to a different sheet in a worksheet:** To access the other sheet, click the sheet tab. If the tab you want isn't visible, use the tab scrolling buttons to bring it up, then click it.

iv. **In a workbook, select the following sheets:** When you choose several sheets, Microsoft Excel duplicates the changes you make to the active sheet on all other pages. Other sheets' data may be replaced as a result of these modifications.

Criteria for selection	Key sequences
A single sheet	Click the sheet tab.
Two or more adjacent sheets	Hold down SHIFT and click the tab for the first sheet, then click the tab for the last sheet.
Two or more sheets that are not adjacent	Hold CTRL and click the tabs for the additional sheets after clicking the first sheet's tab.
A workbook's entire set of sheets	Select All Sheets from the shortcut menu by right-clicking a sheet tab.

v. **Display more or fewer sheet tabs:**

a) Select the tab split bar.

b) Drag the tab split bar to the right or left when the pointer changes to a split pointer, and then use the tab scrolling buttons to scroll through the sheet tabs. Double-click the tab split bar to reset it to its default position.

vi. **Add a new worksheet:**

a) To add a single worksheet, go to the Insert menu and select Worksheet.

b) Hold SHIFT and click the number of worksheet tabs you want to create in the open workbook to add multiple worksheets. Then, under the Insert menu, select Worksheet.

c) Create a new sheet based on a customized template. You must already have a custom sheet template set up.

d) Click Insert after right-clicking a sheet tab.

e) Double-click the sheet-type template you want to use.

vii. **Move or copy sheets:**

Careful: When moving or copying sheets, be cautious. If you move a worksheet, calculations or charts relying on the data on the worksheet may become wrong. Similarly, data on a worksheet may be incorporated in the computation if it is moved across sheets referenced to by a 3-D formula reference.

a) Open the workbook that will receive the sheets if you want to move or copy sheets to it.

b) Select the sheets you want to move or copy by switching to the workbook that contains them.

c) Select Move or Copy Sheet from the Edit menu.

d) To receive the sheets, click the workbook in the To book box.

e) Click the sheet before which you want to insert the shifted or copied sheets in the before sheet box.

f) Select the Create a copy check box to copy the sheets instead of moving them.

viii. Delete sheets from a workbook:

a) Choose the sheets you need to get dispose of.

b) Select Delete Sheet from the Edit menu.

ix. Change the name of a sheet:

a) To open the sheet tab, double-click it.

b) Replace the existing name with a new one.

x. Hide a sheet:

a) Choose the sheets you want to conceal.

b) Point to Sheet in the Format menu, then click Hide.

xi. Hide a workbook:

a) To begin, open the workbook.

b) Select Hide from the Window menu.

xii. Show a workbook that has been hidden:

a) On the Window menu, click Unhide.

b) Double-click the name of the hidden workbook you want to show in the Unhide workbook box.

xiii. Show a sheet that has been hidden:

a) Point to Sheet in the Format menu, then click Unhide.

b) Double-click the left of the hidden sheet you want to display in the Unhide sheet box.

xiv. Cancel a multiple-sheet selection:

a) Click any unselected sheet in a workbook to cancel a selection of multiple sheets.

b) Right-click the tab of a selected sheet if no unselected sheet is visible. Then, on the shortcut menu, select Ungroup Sheets.

Chapter 2: Editing in Excel

Editing includes modifying the data accessible or already entered, and any data entered sometimes necessitates completing activities with numerous changes such as re-entry, changing the contents, and changing the shape and size of sheets. If you want to perform the assignment with as many possibilities as possible, you should use the official Excel procedures. For your convenience, some of them are discussed here.

- Edit the contents of the cells.

- Cells, rows, and columns can be cleared or deleted.

- Remove any cell's contents, formats, or comments.

- Undo & Redo mistakes.

- Separate text in different cells.

- Replace or find data.

- Text and numbers can be found and replaced.

- Make use of a filtering editing technique.

- Filters can be used to display a subset of rows in a list.

- You can use wildcard characters to find text or numbers.

- Make columns out of copied text data.

2.1 Edit the contents of the cells

The cell can be modified both while entering data and after the data has been entered onto the sheet. The following steps can be taken to accomplish this:

a) Double-click the cell containing the information you want to change.

b) Make any changes to the cell contents.

c) Press ENTER to save your changes. Press ESC to undo your changes.

2.2 Cells, rows, and columns can be cleared or deleted

You may want to delete a specific cell, row, or column in a worksheet at times. It can also be done through the menu, but the following brief procedures will assist you in completing the task in the shortest amount of time with the most relevant information. When you delete a cell in Microsoft Excel, it is removed from the worksheet, and the surrounding cells are shifted to fill the empty area. Clearing cells remove the contents (formulas and data), formats (such as number formats, conditional formats, and borders), and comments from the cells but retain the blank cells on the worksheet.

2.3 Remove any cell's contents, formats, or comments

a) You can clear cells, rows, or columns by selecting them.

b) Select Clear from the Edit menu, then All, Contents, Formats, and Comments.

2.4 Undo & Redo Mistakes

These actions are a great complement to implementing and undoing the previous modifications.

a) UNDO: Click Undo to undo recent actions one by one. To undo many activities at once, choose them from the list by clicking the arrow next to Undo. The selected action, as well as all actions above it, is reversed in Microsoft Excel. Press ESC to cancel an entry in a cell or the formula bar before pressing ENTER.

b) REDO (Repeat the last action): Select Repeat from the Edit menu. The Repeat command becomes Can't Repeat if the previous action cannot be repeated.

2.5 Separate text in different cells

This option helps you to enter the regular data on a sheet in the same cell as long as you wish (not more than 32000 spaces). After entering the data in the same cell, it can be formatted with specified width, and it will automatically separate in different cells. It is much useful for importing the data from any text file or any other source and thereafter format in desired cell locations. These can be done by the following:

a) Choose the cell range that contains the text values.

The range can be as long as you want it to be, but it can only be one column wide.

b) Select Text to Columns from the Data menu.

c) To specify how you wish to divide the text into columns, use the Convert Text to Columns Wizard's instructions. (It will assist you through the task in three steps.)

2.6 Replace or find data

You can look for specific text or numbers that you want to review or amend, and you can have the data you find immediately replaced. You can alternatively choose all the cells that contain the same type of data as the active cell, such as equations, or cells whose contents differ from the active cell. Similar steps in WORD can be used to get these outcomes. Find aids in the discovery of data based on matching criteria, whereas replacing aids in the discovery of data and its replacement with the specified altered version. Filters can be used to display just the rows in a list that have the requested data. You can, for example, present only local sales data in a list that contains international sales data.

2.7 Text and numbers can be found and replaced

Under this, you can use this option to find & replace text or numbers, select blank cells. Select cells that contain constants comments that don't match active cells etc. It is much powerful to perform the task as a sheet navigator.

2.8 Make use of a filtering editing technique

You can use it to filter a list to find certain rows of data.

Cells that meet certain criteria are highlighted.

a) Choose the cells you want to draw attention to.

b) Select Conditional Formatting from the Format menu.

c) Choose one of the following options:

i. Click Cell Value is, pick the comparison phrase, and then type a value in the relevant box to use values in the selected cells as the formatting criteria. A constant value or a formula can be entered. If you're going to enter a formula, make sure it starts with an equal sign (=).

ii. Click Formula Is on the left, then input the formula in the box on the right to use a formula as the formatting criterion (to evaluate data or a condition other than the values in selected cells). The formula must return TRUE or FALSE as a logical value.

d) Click format

e) Choose the font style, color, underlining, borders, shading, or patterns you'd want to use. Only if the cell value matches the criterion or if the formula returns TRUE does Excel apply the selected formats.

f) Click Add to add another condition, then repeat steps 3 through 5 to add another condition.

2.9 Display a subset of rows in a list by using filters

Filters can only be applied to one worksheet at a time. Only one list on a worksheet can be filtered at a time.

a) To filter a cell in a list, click it.

b) Point to Filter on the Data menu, then click AutoFilter.

c) To display only the rows with a given value, click the arrow in the column containing the information you want to display.

d) Click the value.

e) Repeat steps 3 and 4 in the other column to apply an additional condition based on a value in that column.

Click the arrow in the column, then click Custom to filter the list by two values in the same column or to use comparison operators other than Equals. Click here for more information on displaying rows by comparing values.

2.10 You can use wildcard characters to find text or numbers

Use a wildcard character to identify text or numbers that share some characters or digits. One or more unidentified characters are represented by a wildcard character.

Use	To Find
? (question mark)	Any single character in the same position as the question mark. For example, smith finds "smith" and "Smyth."
*(asterisk)	In the same position as the asterisk, any number of characters can be used. * east, for example, will return "Northeast" and "Southeast."
~(tilde) followed by? *,~	A tilde, an asterisk, or a question mark. fy91, for example, finds "fy91?"

2.11 Make columns out of copied text data

a) Change to the program and file where you want to copy data from.

b) Select the data you want to copy

c) Select Copy from the Edit menu of the program.

d) Switch to your Microsoft Excel workbook, choose the upper-left cell in the paste area, and then press the Paste button.

e) Choose the cell range that contains the pasted data. The range can be as long as you want it to be, but it can only be one column wide.

f) On the Data menu, click Text to Columns.

g) Choose the cell range that contains the pasted data. The range can be as long as you want it to be, but it can only be one column wide.

Chapter 3: Working with Charts

One picture is supposed to be worth a thousand words. Charts are essential for the analytical display of data in any do present system. If you are well-versed in statistics and believe in the analysis and management aspects, you can experiment with the excel charting system, which displays the last touch of any data analysis system. To finish the assignment, you must first prepare the data, which is an important aspect of any business or corporate model. If you're new to Excel, go over the basics in a more compact manner, such as establishing a chance.

You will be able to complete the following subjects after going through this chapter:

- Why are Charts used?
- The fundamental idea.
- Elements of a Chart.
- Various types of Charts.
- Creating a Chart.
- Create a chart in one step.
- Make a chart out of non-adjacent selections.
- Select a different chart type.
- Saving & Retrieval of Charts.

3.1 Why Charts are used?

Charts are visually appealing and make patterns, data comparisons, and trends easy to notice for consumers. Instead of studying multiple columns of spreadsheet numbers, you may see whether embedded sales are dropping or rising over time, or how all actual sales compare to projected sales, all at a glance. A chart can be produced as a separate sheet or as an item embedded within a spreadsheet. A chart can be incorporated in a Web page as well. Before you can design the chart, you must first enter the data for it on the worksheet. Then, using the Chart Wizard, select the chart type and as part of the numerous chart types.

3.2 The fundamental idea

Some data models can be used to make charts. If you're not familiar with the details, consider that a comprehensive data model can display all of the charts, both embedded and non-embedded. If it is embedded, the chart's mapping will be modified automatically after the data is entered. You may make charts in Excel using wizards or by following the methods laid forth in the program. The following details are critical for any chart that represents a system.

a) **Worksheet data and chart:** Without utilizing the Chart Wizard, you may make a chart in one step. The chart utilizes a default chart type and formatting when produced this way, which you can adjust later. Worksheet data is represented as a chart; the chart is linked to the worksheet data and is automatically created and updated when the worksheet data is changed. The following tables are used to create the chart's appearance.

3.3 Elements of a Chart

a) **Axis Value:** The axis values are generated by Microsoft Excel using the worksheet data. In the example above, the axis values run from 0 to 9000, which covers the whole range of values on the worksheet. Unless you indicate otherwise, Excel uses the number format for the axis from the upper-left cell in the value range.

b) **Names of data series in the chart:** Excel also uses row or column headings in the worksheet data for series names. Series names appear in the chart legend. You can change whether Excel uses row or column headings for series names or create different names.

c) **In a chart, how is data organized?**

1. **Embedded Charts:** An embedded chart is a graphic item that stores data and can be used as part of the worksheet on which it was generated. When you want to display or print one or more charts with your worksheet data, use embedded charts.

2. **Embedded charts and Chart Sheets:** A chart can be created on its own chart sheet or as an embedded chart on a

worksheet. In either case, the chart is linked to the worksheet's source data, so it is updated when the worksheet is updated.

3. **Chart Sheets:** A chart sheet is a distinct sheet with its own name within your workbook. When you want to see or update large or complex charts independently from the worksheet data or save screen space while working on the worksheet, use a chart sheet.

d) **Category Names:** For category axis names, Excel employs row or column headings in the worksheet data. The worksheet row headers 1st Quarter, 2nd Quarter, and likewise appear as category axis names in the sample above. For category axis names, you can choose whether Excel utilizes column or row headers, or you can make up your own.

e) **Data Markers:** One data series is represented by data markers with the same pattern. Each data marker corresponds to one of the worksheet's numbers.

3.4 Various Type of Charts

In Excel, there are 14 different types of charts, each of which is broken into sub-categories called sub-segments. Each chart type can be used to illustrate any form of business data. The

most common types of charts in Excel are described in this heading.

Below, we'll go through some key points regarding these charts:

a) **Bar:** A bar chart depicts comparisons between different items. To focus on comparing values and lay less emphasis on time, categories are grouped vertically, and values are organized horizontally. Individual items' relationships to the total are depicted using stacked bar charts.

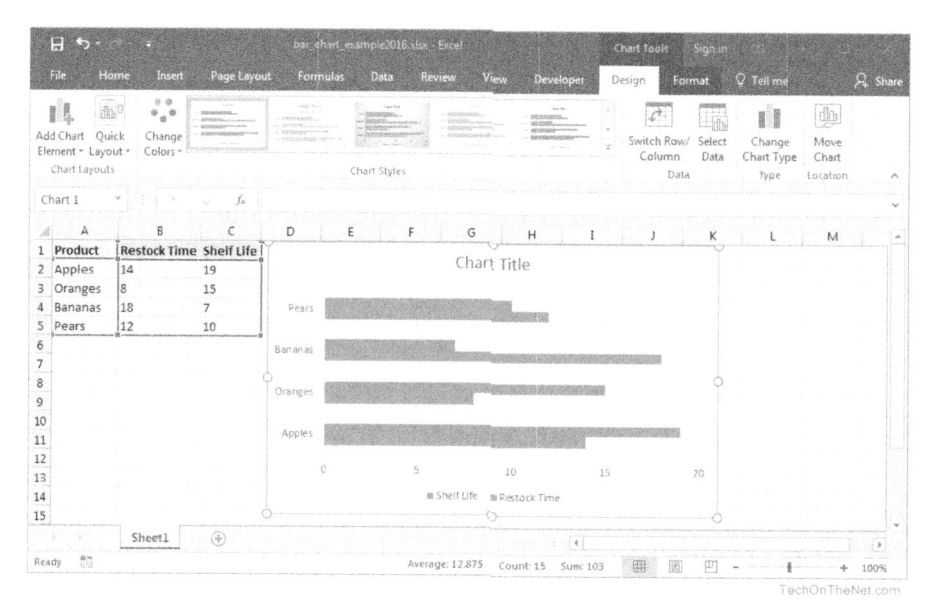

b) **Stock:** A stock chart with a volume axis has two value axes: one for the volume columns and the other for the stock prices. A high-low-close or open-high-low-close chart might contain volume.

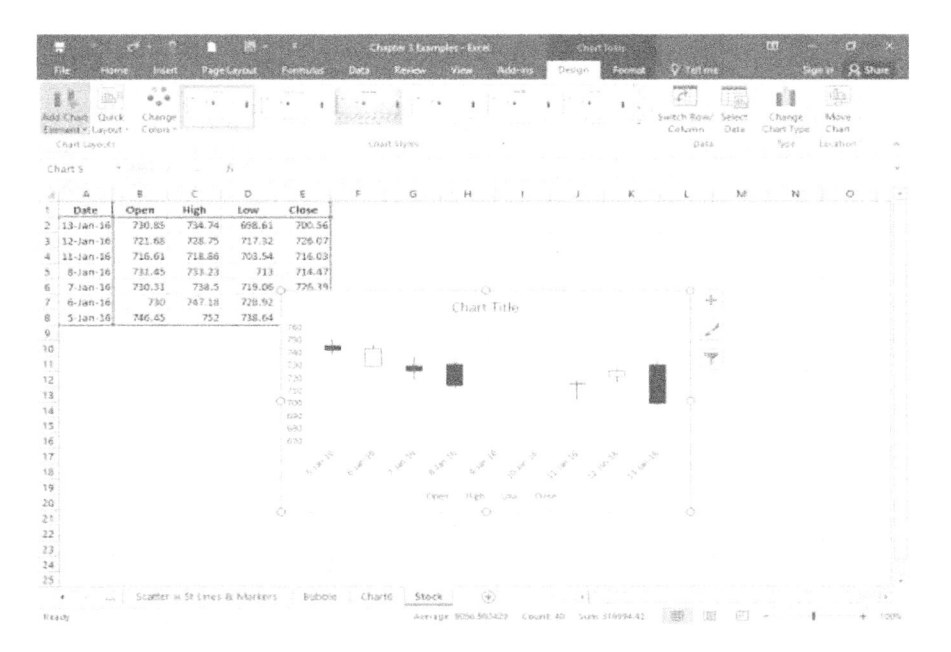

c) **Surface:** When you need to determine the best combinations of two sets of data, a surface chart comes in handy. Colours and patterns, just like on a topographic map, identify areas with similar values. This graph depicts the numerous temperature and time combinations that result in the same tensile strength measurement. You have the option of selecting any type of chart before and after the data, the model is created. In the case of comprehensive data generation, adding the element of charts for additional display can be beneficial.

d) **Column:** A column chart depicts changes in data over time or highlights comparisons between things. To emphasize variation across time, categories are grouped horizontally, and values are organized vertically. Individual items' relationships to the total are depicted in stacked column charts. Data points are compared along two axes in the 3-D perspective column chart. You may compare the performance of four quarters of sales in Europe with the performance of two other divisions in this 3-D chart.

e) **Doughnut:** A doughnut chart, like a pie chart, depicts the relationship between portions and the whole, but it can hold multiple data series. A data series is represented by each ring of the doughnut chart. The high-low-close chart is a popular way to depict stock prices. This chart can also be used to represent scientific data, such as temperature variations. To produce this and other stock charts, you must first organize your data in the correct sequence.

f) **XY (Scatter):** An XY (scatter) chart depicts the relationships between numeric values in multiple data series or plots two groups of numbers as a single XY coordinate series. This chart, which depicts data in irregular intervals or clusters, is widely used for scientific data. Place x values in one row or column, then corresponding y values in adjacent rows or columns when arranging your data. Cone, cylinder, and pyramid data markers can give 3-D column and bar charts a dramatic effect.

3.5 Creating a Chart

Either an embedded chart or a chart sheet can be created.

a) Select the cells that contain the data you want to see in the chart. Include the cells that contain the column and row labels in the selection if you want them to appear in the chart.

b) Click Chart Wizard.

c) Follow the instructions in chart wizard.

3.6 Create a Chart in one step

a) Select the data you want to plot and then press F11 to create a chart sheet with the default chart type.

b) Select the data you want to plot and then click Default Chart to create an embedded chart that utilizes the default chart type. Add the Default Chart button to a toolbar if it isn't already there.

3.7 Make a chart out of non-adjacent selections

a) Choose the first set of cells in the table that contain the information you want to add.

b) Select any more cell groupings you want to include while holding CTRL. A rectangle must be formed by the nonadjacent selections.

c) Click Chart Wizard

d) Follow the instructions in the Chart Wizard.

3.8 Select a different chart type

You can alter the chart type of a data series or the entire chart in most 2-D charts. You can only modify the type of the entire chart with bubble charts. Changing the chart type impacts the entire chart in most 3-D graphics. A data series can be changed to a cylinder, cone, or pyramid chart type for 3-D column and bar charts.

a) Choose one of the following options:

Click the chart to change the chart type for the entire chart.

To change the chart type of a data series, click the data series.

b) Select Chart Type from the Chart menu.

c) Select the chart type you want from the Standard Types or Custom Types tabs.

To apply the cylinder, cone, or pyramid chart type to a 3-D column and bar data series, choose the Apply to selection check box and then click Cone, Cylinder, or Pyramid in the Chart type box on the Standard Types tab.

3.9 Saving & Retrieval of Charts

It's similar to completing the operation of creating, saving, and retrieving data and charts all at once without exerting additional effort because the sheet will be automatically recovered while recovering it. After providing more efficient views, you can see that when you invoke the graph, it creates a new sheet with the name chart, and altering the type increases the number of chart sheets. There are other features available in Excel, such as pivot tables and online forms, that must be discussed.

Chapter 4: Advanced Data Retrieval

We'll talk about the database capabilities of Excel in this chapter, which allow data access much more trustworthy with the help of various office tools. Each section's specifics are detailed in detail for your convenience. You will be able to master the following details after completing this session:

- Pivot Table.
- Creation of a pivot table report.
- Deletion of a pivot table report.
- Query.
- How to retrieve data?

4.1 Pivot Table

A Pivot Table report is an interactive table that may be used to summarise vast amounts of data quickly. You can rotate the rows and columns to get multiple summaries of the source data, filter the data by viewing different pages, and view details for specific areas of interest. The following information is primarily provided to help you comprehend the concept, purpose, and other associated aspects.

a) **When should a Pivot Table report be used:** When you need to compare related totals, a Pivot Table report comes in handy, especially when you have a long list of statistics to summarise and compare numerous facts about each figure.

When you want Microsoft Excel to conduct the sorting, subtotalling, and totalling, use Pivot Table reports. You or other users can change the view of the data in a Pivot Table report since it is interactive.

b) **Creating a PivotTable report:** Use the PivotTable and PivotChart Wizard as a guide to find and specify the source data you wish to analyze and to build the report structure for a PivotTable report. The Pivot Table toolbar can then be used to arrange the data within that framework.

c) **Types of pivot table report:** The following is an example of a standard Pivot Table report. You may also view all the summary figures of the same type in one column by displaying a PivotTable report in indented format. To see the data graphically, you can build a PivotChart report. When you publish an Excel Pivot Table report to a Pivot Table list on a Web page, others can view and interact with the data from their Web browsers.

d) **Source data for a Pivot Table report:** A Pivot Table report can be created using a Microsoft Excel list, Excel worksheets from an external database, or another Pivot Table report. To compare the multiple presentations of the same data, the following source data is utilized for the rest of the sample reports on this topic.

e) **How to set up the source data:** Rows and columns are used to organize data from Excel lists and most databases. Similar facts in the same column must appear in your source data. The region for sale is always in column E in the example, the quantity sold is in column D, and so on.

f) **OLAP source data:** Instead of rows and columns, OLAP databases aggregate enormous volumes of data into dimensions and levels. Because the OLAP server calculates the summary values for the PivotTable report rather than Excel, you can use PivotTable reports to display and analyze data from OLAP databases. Data retrieval from an OLAP database is more efficient, and you can analyze larger amounts of data than you can with other types of databases. Excel also allows you to create OLAP cubes from data in external databases and save them as cube files so you may work with them offline.

g) **Field and items:** Each field in a PivotTable report corresponds to a column (or OLAP dimension) in the source data and summarises rows of data from the source data. A PivotTable report's fields list data objects across rows or down columns. The cells at the intersection of the rows and columns provide summarised data for the items at the top of the column and on the left side of the row.

h) **Data Fields and Cells:** The values that are summarised in the Pivot table report are provided by a data field, such as Sum of Sales.

i) **Summary Functions:** Pivot Table reports use summary functions like Sum, Count, or Average to summarise the data field values. These functions also automatically generate subtotals and grand totals if you desire to display them. The data from the Sales column in the source list is summed in this example with the sum, which displays subtotals for the months as well as grand totals for the rows and columns.

j) **Viewing details:** You may see the detail rows from the source data that make up the summary value in a single data cell in most PivotTable reports. Although OLAP source data is not arranged in rows that can be viewed in this manner, you can adjust the amount of detail presented throughout the PivotTable report if it is based on OLAP source data.

k) **Changing the layout:** You can see your data in multiple ways and calculate different summarised results by dragging a field button to another portion of the Pivot Table report. For example, instead of looking down the rows, you can see the names of salespeople across the columns. By dragging a field or item, you can adjust the report layout.

l) **Elements of Pivot Table report:** The indented format of a Pivot Table report is comparable to that of a standard database banded report or prepared report. The data for each row field is indented in a text outline-like manner. You can read all of the summarised figures for a data field along a single column using this style. It's great for extended reports or reports that need to be printed out.

m) **Graphical views of Pivot Table data:** A PivotChart report, like a Pivot Table report, is an interactive chart that you can use to see and rearrange data graphically. A PivotChart report is always accompanied by a Pivot Table report in the same workbook, which contains all of the associated report's source data. A PivotChart report, like a Pivot Table report, contains field buttons that you can utilize to adjust the layout and display various data.

n) **Pivot Table lists on the web:** A Pivot Table report can be saved as a Web page and then published to a public site, such as a Web server. The report is known as a Pivot Table list there, and it has a lot of the same interactive features as the report in Microsoft Excel. Other users having the Microsoft Office Web Components installed can view and interact with the PivotTable list using the Microsoft Internet Explorer Web browser version 4.01 or later. Users can install the Office Web Components by installing Microsoft Office or by downloading the Office Web Components from their business intranet if their employer has an Office site license.

o) **Row Fields:** In a PivotTable report, fields from the underlying source data are allocated a row orientation. As an example, consider the following. Row fields include Product and Sold By. When a Pivot Table report has more than one-row field, the one closest to the data area is the inner row field. Outer row fields refer to any remaining row fields. The properties of the inner and outer row fields are different. The items in the outermost field are only shown once; however, the remainder of the fields are repeated as needed.

p) **Column Field:** In a Pivot Table report, a field with a column orientation. As an example, consider the following. Qtr2 and Qtr3 are two fields in the Quarters column. Multiple critical pieces of information can be included in a Pivot Table report. It can have column fields just like it can have row fields. Column fields are not available in most Pivot Table reports with an indented structure.

q) **Item:** A Pivot Table field's subcategory or member. Dairy and Meat are items in the Product field in the preceding example. Items in the source data indicate unique entries in the same field or column. Items appear as row or column labels, as well as in page field drop-down menus.

r) **Page Field:** A field that is assigned to the orientation of a page or filter. The region is a page field in this example that you may use to filter the report by region. You can display summarised statistics for only the East area, only the West region, or for all regions using the Region option. When you select a different item in a page field, the Pivot Table report changes to only show the summarised data for that item.

s) **Page Field Item:** In the page field list, each unique entry or value from the field, or column, in the source list or table becomes an item as an example. The East region is currently selected in the Region page field, and the PivotTable report only shows data for that region.

t) **Data Field:** A field that includes data to be summarised from a source list or database. As an example. Sum of Sales is a data field that sums up the entries in the source data's Sales field or column. This field is called Sales instead of Sum of Sales in the indented-format report example.

The underlying data in a data field is commonly numeric data, such as statistics or sales numbers, but it can also be text. By default, Microsoft Excel uses the Count summary function to summarise text data in Pivot Table reports and Sum to summarise numeric data.

u) **Data area:** A summary data section in a Pivot Table report. The elements in the row and column fields are summarised in the data area's cells. Each value in the data area is a summary of information from the source records or rows.

v) **Field drop-down arrow:** Each field has an arrow on the right side. Select the items you wish to show by clicking this arrow.

The field arrow displays only the highest level field in a dimension in PivotTable reports that are based on source data from OLAP databases, and you can choose items at multiple levels in the field. When you click the drop-down arrow for a Year field, you may see the following.

w) **Expand Indicator:** The or symbol next to the items in a field. To show or hide detail for an item, click the indicator for the item.

4.2 Creation of a pivot table report

a) You may want to retrieve data before creating a Pivot Table report that is based on external on-OLAP source data.

- Open the workbook in which the Pivot Table report will be created.

- Click a cell in the list or database if the report is based on a Microsoft Excel list or database.

- Select Pivot Table and PivotChart Report from the Data menu.

- Follow the instructions in Step 1 of the Pivot Table and PivotChart Wizard, and then click Pivot Table under What sort of report do you want to create?

- Follow the wizard's instructions in step 2.

- Determine whether you need to click Layout in the wizard's third step.

- Do one of the following:

When you've finished putting out the report in the wizard, click OK in the Pivot Table and PivotChart Wizard-Layout dialogue box, then Finish finish creating the report if you choose Layout in step 3.

If you skipped Step 3 and didn't click Layout, click Finish and then lay out the report on the spreadsheet.

b) **Using an existing Pivot Table or Pivot Chart Report:** You can use an existing PivotTable report to create a new PivotTable report, but you can't use an existing PivotChart report to create a new PivotChart report. You may, however, base a new Pivot Table or PivotChart report on the associated Pivot Table report because Excel creates one whenever you create a PivotChart report.

c) **Changes that affect both reports:** Microsoft Excel automatically updates the data in the old report on which the new report is based when you refresh the data in the new Pivot Table or PivotChart report, and vice versa. Both are affected when you group or ungroup data in a single report. Both reports are affected when you generate calculated fields or calculated items in one report.

d) **Requirements for location:** Both reports must be in the same workbook to use a PivotTable report to build another PivotTable or Pivot Chart report. Copy the original Pivot Table report to the workbook where you want the new report to display if it's in a separate worksheet. Each PivotTable and PivotChart report in a distinct workbook has its own intermediary copy of the data in memory and in the workbook file, allowing you to refresh the reports independently.

e) **Page Field Setting:** Any page fields that are set to query for external data as you select each item cannot be found in the initial Pivot Table report.

f) **Pivot Table reports that are independent of Pivot Chart report:** Changes to a Pivot Chart report have an impact on the Pivot Table report that it is linked to and vice versa. You can construct a separate independent Pivot Table report if you wish to be able to change the style or display different data without affecting both reports.

g) **Create a Pivot Chart Report:** Microsoft Excel automatically creates a Pivot Table report when you create a PivotChart report. If you already have a Pivot Table report, you can use it to produce a Pivot Chart report that reflects the table's view. When creating a PivotChart report based on external on-OLAP source data, you may need to retrieve the external data first. Open the workbook where the PivotChart report will be created.

Click a cell in the list or database if the report is based on an Excel list or database.

- Select Pivot Table and PivotChart Report from the Data menu.

- Follow the steps in Step 1 of the Pivot Table and PivotChart Wizard, and then click PivotChart (under What sort of report do you want to create?)

- Follow the instructions in step 2 of the wizard.

- In step 3 of the wizard, specify where you want to put the associated Pivot Table report. The PivotChart report is automatically created on a new chart sheet. Then determine whether you need to click Layout.

- Do one of the following.

If you selected layout in step 3 of the process, click OK in the Layout dialogue box after laying out the PivotChart report in the wizard, and then click Finish to create the PivotChart report.

If you skipped step 3 of the wizard and didn't click Layout, click Finish and then lay out the PivotChart report on the chart sheet.

4.3 Deletion of a Pivot Table report

a) Click the Pivot Table report.

b) Click PivotTable in the Pivot Table toolbar, point to Select and then click Entire Table.

c) Point to Clear on the Edit menu, then click All.

The preceding information is enough to grasp the comprehensive handling of Pivot table elements across all systems. The following are the shortcut key combinations for using the pivot table option:

Key Sequence Required	Function
UP ARROW or DOWN ARROW	In the list, click the previous or next field button.
LEFT ARROW or RIGHT ARROW	In a multicolumn field button list, select the field button on the left or right.
ALT+C Move the	The selected field into the column area
ALT+D Move the	The selected field into the data area
ALT+L	The Pivot Table Field dialogue box appears.

ALT+P	Insert the chosen field into the Page area.
ALT+R	Place the chosen field in the Row area.

a) Layout keys for PivotTable and PivotChart reports:

- To activate the menu bar, press F10.

- To access the Pivot Table toolbar, use CTRL+TAB or CTRL+SHIFT+TAB.

- To select the menu to the left or right, or to switch between the main menu and a submenu, press the LEFT ARROW or RIGHT ARROW keys.

- To select the area to which you desire to relocate the selected field, press ENTER (on a field button) and the DOWN ARROW and UP ARROW keys.

b) Grouping and Ungrouping Pivot Table Items:

Key Sequence required Function

ALT+SHIFT+RIGHT ARROW   Group select Pivot Table items

ALT+ SHIFT+LEFT ARROW   Ungroup selected Pivot Table items

c) Menus and Toolbar:

Key Sequence Required	Function
F10 or ALT	Make the menu bar active, or simultaneously close a visible menu and submenu.
TAB or SHIFT+TAB	On the toolbar, select the next or previous button or menu (when a toolbar is active).
CTRL+TAB or CTRL+SHIFT+TAB	Switch between the next and previous toolbars (when a toolbar is active).
ENTER	Open the menu you've selected, or conduct out the action you've assigned to the button you've selected.
SHIFT+F10	Show a shortcut menu
ALT+SPACEBAR	Show the icon menu for the program (on the program title bar).

DOWN ARROW or UP ARROW	On the menu or submenu, select the next or previous command (with the menu or submenu displayed).
LEFT ARROW or RIGHT ARROW	Select the menu to the left or right, or move between the main menu and the submenu if a submenu is visible.
HOME or END	On the menu or submenu, select the first or last command.
ESC	Close the visible menu or close the submenu only if a submenu is visible.
CTRL+DOWN ARROW	On a menu, show the entire list of commands.

4.4 QUERY: A Reliable inquiry counter

Microsoft Query is an application that allows you to import data from a variety of sources into Microsoft Excel. You won't have to retype the data you want to examine in Excel if you use Query to retrieve data from your company databases and files. You can also have your Excel reports and summaries updated automatically whenever the original source database is updated with fresh data.

a) **Types of databases you can access:** Microsoft Access, Microsoft SQL Server, and Microsoft SQL Server OLAP Services are all examples of WORKING WITH CHARTS databases from which you can retrieve data. Data can also be retrieved from Excel spreadsheets and text files. You can also get data from Web pages in Excel, but you don't need Query to do so.

b) **Selecting data from a database:** A query, which is a question regarding data stored in an external database, is used to get data from a database. You might want to know the sales figures for a given product by region if your data is housed in an access database. You can retrieve only the data you need by selecting only the data for the product and region you want to study and ignoring the rest. With Query, you can select and choose whatever columns of data you want to bring into Excel.

c) **Updating your worksheet in one operation:** When you have external data in an Excel worksheet, you may refresh the data to update your analysis without having to rewrite your summary reports and charts anytime your database changes. You could, for example, construct a monthly sales summary and update it every month when new sales statistics arrive.

d) **Retrieving data via Query:** There are three steps to bringing outer data into Excel using Query To connect to your database, first create a data source, then utilize the Query Wizard to choose the data you want, and lastly, return the data to Excel to format, summarise, and make reports from it.

e) **What is the definition of a data source?** A data source is a set of data that Microsoft Excel uses to connect to an external database. When you use Microsoft Query to create a data source, you give it a name and then specify the database or server's name and location, the database type, and your log-on and password information. The data also includes the name of an ODBC driver, also known as a data source driver, which is a program that connects to a specific database type. To retrieve data from various types of external databases, all you have to do is create a data source.

f) **How Microsoft Query works with data sources:** Once you've created a data source for a database, you can use it to select and retrieve data from that database without having to retype all of the connection information. The data source is used by Query to connect to an external database and display the data that is accessible. Query obtains the data and sends the query and data source information to the Excel workbook so you may reconnect to the database when you wish to refresh the data after you build your query and return the data to Excel. A data source is a method by which Query and Excel connect to a database and obtain information from it.

4.5 How to Retrieve Data

a) **Use the Query Wizard for all the queries:** The Query Wizard, that is included in Microsoft Query, is intended for customers who are unfamiliar with query creation. The wizard simplifies the process of selecting and combining data from various tables and fields in your database. You can also use the wizard to filter and sort the results of your query after you've selected the data you want. The Query Wizard can be used to build a complete query or to start a query that you can modify directly in Query.

You can work straight in Query if you're experienced with query creation or wish to develop a more complicated query. You can use Query to view and modify queries you started in the Query Wizard, or you can use it to generate new queries without using it.

b) **Use Query directly when you want to create queries that do the following:**

- Choose specific information from a field. You may want to choose some of the data in a field and leave out data you don't need in a large database. For instance, if you require data for two of the items in a field with a large number of products.

- Each time you run the query, it will return data based on different criteria. You can make a parameter query if you need to create the same Excel report or summary for several places in the same external data, such as a distinct sales report for each region. When you run a parameter query, you'll be asked for the data that will be used as the criteria for selecting records. A parameter query, for example, would ask you to enter a certain region, and you could reuse this query to build each of your regional sales reports.

- Data can be combined in a variety of ways. You can use Query to join data from different tables in your database by combining them. For example, if you have a database of product sales data and a table of customer data, you could link the two records to display customers who haven't made a purchase in a while.

- These options are mostly for analysis and calculation wizards for the most efficient operation of computing demands according to organizational structure.

Chapter 5: Functions

Functions have emerged to perform the functional responsibilities for any application, and they are extremely important in Excel. It saves time by eliminating the need to perform complex calculations for any study or query that requires future-based results.

Functions are established formulas that execute calculations by combining certain values (arguments) in a precise order (syntax). The SUM function, for example, adds values or cell ranges. Let's say you wanted to add a list of 100 integers in a column, starting at cell Al and ending at cell A100. You wouldn't be able to enter 100 different additions in a cell even if you wanted to since you'd run out of space. Simply put, a function = SUM can be entered (A1:A100). So, given the arguments A1, A2, A3, and A100, the sum function will return the addition of 100 values. Numbers, text, logical values like TRUE or FALSE, arrays, error values like #N/A, and cell references can all be used as arguments. You must specify an argument that produces a valid value for that argument. Constants, formulae, and other functions can also be used as arguments.

5.1 Date & Time Functions

Excel has a number of features for working with times and dates.

1. NOW & TODAY

2. DATE, DAY, MONTH and YEAR

3. TIME, HOUR, MINUTE and SECOND

4. DATEDIF & YEARFRAC

5. EDATE & EOMONTH

6. WORKDAY & NETWORKDAYS

7. WEEKDAY & WEEKNUM

Here's a brief overview of some of the most important Excel functions to remember.

1. NOW & TODAY

TODAY function and the NOW function can be used to get the present day and time. Since the NOW function technically returns the current date & time, you can format it as a time only, as seen below:

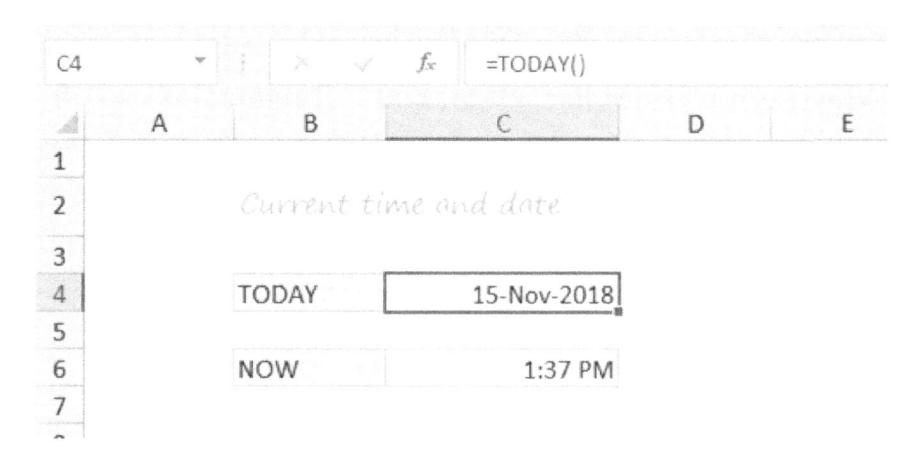

	A	B	C	D	E
1					
2		*Current time and date*			
3					
4		TODAY	15-Nov-2018		
5					
6		NOW	1:37 PM		
7					

- **NOW ()** RETURNS CURRENT DATE
- **TODAY ()** RETURNS CURRENT DATE

Note: These are volatile functions, which means they can recalculate every time the worksheet is changed. Using date & time shortcuts if you want a constant value.

2. **DATE, DAY, MONTH and YEAR**

You can disassemble whatever date into its raw components with the DAY, MONTH, and YEAR functions and then reassemble it with the DATE function.

	A	B	C	D	E	F	G	H
1								
2		Take dates apart and put them back together again						
3								
4		Date		YEAR	MONTH	DAY		DATE
5		14-Nov-18		2018	11	14		14-Nov-18
6		23-Apr-12		2012	4	23		23-Apr-12
7		20-Feb-00		2000	2	20		20-Feb-00
8		4-Oct-95		1995	10	4		4-Oct-95

H5 f_x =DATE(D5,E5,F5)

=**DATE** (2018,11,14) // returns 14-Nov-2018

=**DAY** ("14 Nov 2018") // returns 14

=**MONTH** ("14 Nov 2018") // returns 11

=**YEAR** ("14 Nov 2018") // returns 2018

3. TIME, HOUR, MINUTE and SECOND

Excel has a number of time-related parallel functions. You can extract pieces of time using the HOUR, MINUTE, and SECOND functions, and you can generate a TIME from individual components using the TIME function.

	A	B	C	D	E	F	G	H
1								
2		*Take times apart and put them back together again*						
3								
4		Date		HOUR	MINUTE	SECOND		TIME
5		10:00 AM	-->	10	0	0	-->	10:00 AM
6		11:30 AM	-->	11	30	0	-->	11:30 AM
7		3:05:02	-->	3	5	2	-->	3:05:02
8		5:15 PM	-->	17	15	0	-->	5:15 PM
9								

H5 =TIME(D5,E5,F5)

=TIME (10,30,0) // returns 10:30

=HOUR ("10:30") // returns 10

=MINUTE ("10:30") // returns 30

=SECOND ("10:30") // returns 0

4. DATEDIF & YEARFRAC

DATEDIF function can be used to calculate the period between two dates in years, in months, or in days. DATEDIF may also be set up to calculate cumulative duration in "normalized" measures, such as "2 years, 6 months, and 27 days."

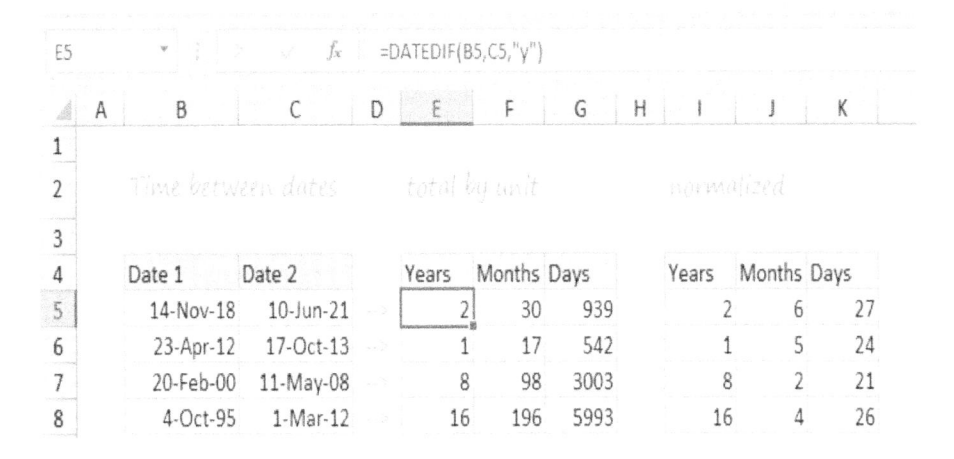

	A	B	C	D	E	F	G	H	I	J	K
1											
2		*Time between dates*			*total by unit*				*normalized*		
3											
4		Date 1	Date 2		Years	Months	Days		Years	Months	Days
5		14-Nov-18	10-Jun-21		2	30	939		2	6	27
6		23-Apr-12	17-Oct-13		1	17	542		1	5	24
7		20-Feb-00	11-May-08		8	98	3003		8	2	21
8		4-Oct-95	1-Mar-12		16	196	5993		16	4	26

E5: `=DATEDIF(B5,C5,"y")`

To get fractional years, use YEARFRAC:

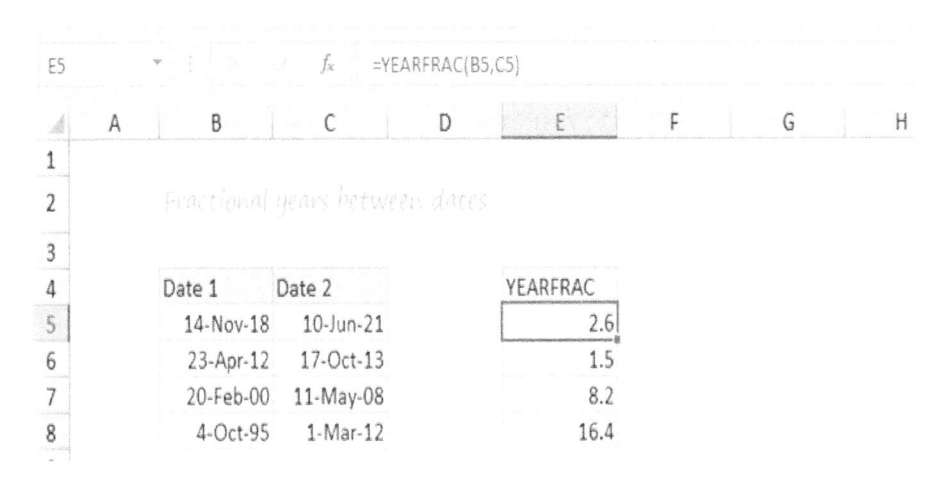

	A	B	C	D	E	F	G	H
1								
2		*Fractional years between dates*						
3								
4		Date 1	Date 2		YEARFRAC			
5		14-Nov-18	10-Jun-21		2.6			
6		23-Apr-12	17-Oct-13		1.5			
7		20-Feb-00	11-May-08		8.2			
8		4-Oct-95	1-Mar-12		16.4			

E5: `=YEARFRAC(B5,C5)`

= **YEARFRAC** ("14 Nov 2018","10 Jun 2021") // returns 2.57

5. EDATE & EOMONTH

Shifting a date forward or backward by a certain no. of months is a typical task for dates. You can do this with the EDATE & EOMONTH functions. EDATE keeps the day and shifts by month. The same is true for EOMONTH, except that it still returns last day of the month.

	A	B	C	D	E	F	G
1							
2		Shift dates forward or backward by months					
3							
4		Start	Months		EDATE	EOMONTH	
5		20-Mar-2010	6	-->	20-Sep-2010	30-Sep-2010	
6		11-Aug-2013	-6	-->	11-Feb-2013	28-Feb-2013	
7		30-Nov-2015	12	-->	30-Nov-2016	30-Nov-2016	
8		10-Jan-2017	0	-->	10-Jan-2017	31-Jan-2017	
9		7-May-2018	9	-->	7-Feb-2019	28-Feb-2019	
10		19-Jul-2020	24	-->	19-Jul-2022	31-Jul-2022	

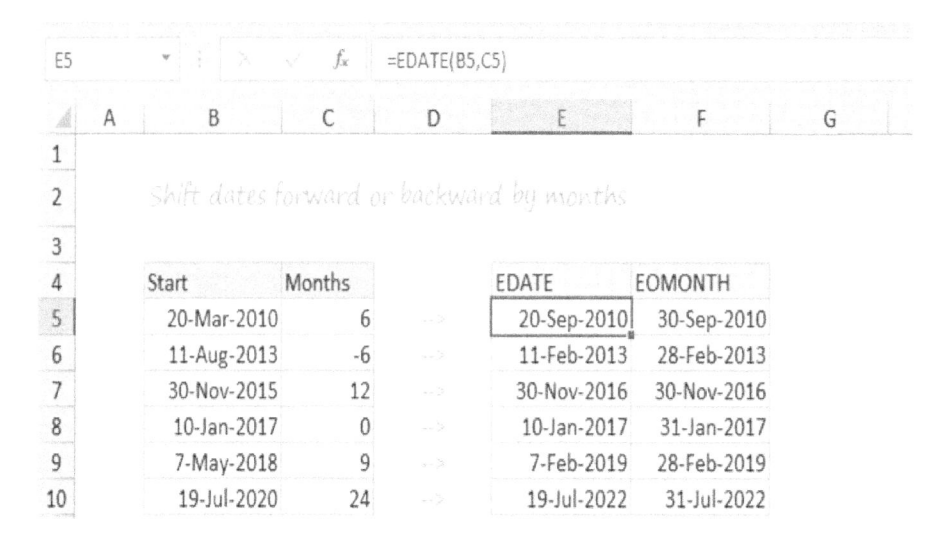

EDATE (date,6) // six months forward

EOMONTH (date,6) // six months forward (end of month)

6. WORKDAY & NETWORKDAYS

The WORKDAY function will be used to calculate a date n workday in the future. NETWORKDAYS may be used to measure the number of workdays between two dates.

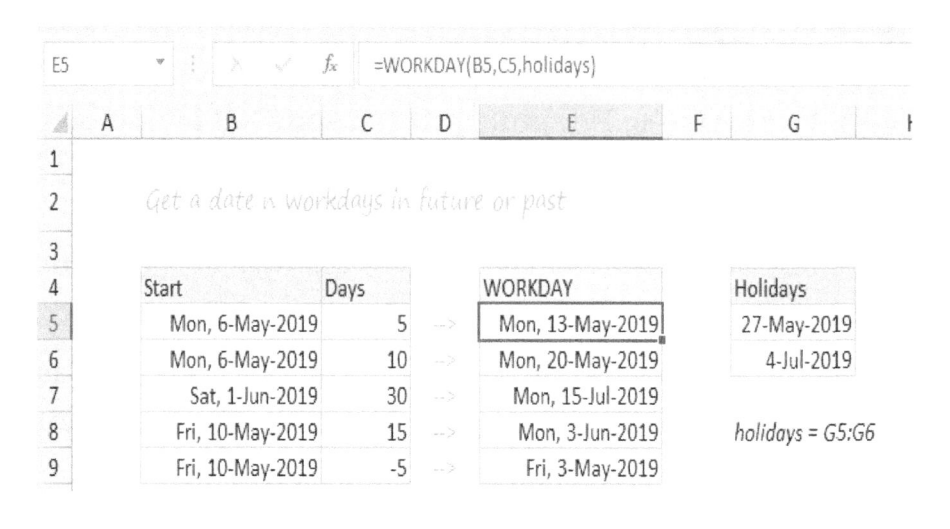

	A	B	C	D	E	F	G
1							
2		Get a date n workdays in future or past					
3							
4		Start	Days		WORKDAY		Holidays
5		Mon, 6-May-2019	5	-->	Mon, 13-May-2019		27-May-2019
6		Mon, 6-May-2019	10	-->	Mon, 20-May-2019		4-Jul-2019
7		Sat, 1-Jun-2019	30	-->	Mon, 15-Jul-2019		
8		Fri, 10-May-2019	15	-->	Mon, 3-Jun-2019		holidays = G5:G6
9		Fri, 10-May-2019	-5	-->	Fri, 3-May-2019		

WORKDAY (start, n, holidays) // date n workdays in future

	A	B	C	D	E	F	G
1							
2		*Get number of workdays between dates*					
3							
4		Start	Finish		Workdays		Holidays
5		Mon, 6-May-2019	Mon, 13-May-2019		6		27-May-2019
6		Mon, 6-May-2019	Mon, 20-May-2019		11		4-Jul-2019
7		Sat, 1-Jun-2019	Mon, 15-Jul-2019		30		
8		Fri, 10-May-2019	Mon, 3-Jun-2019		16		holidays = E5:E6
9		Fri, 10-May-2019	Fri, 3-May-2019		-6		

E5: =NETWORKDAYS(B5,C5,holidays)

NETWORKDAYS (start, end, holidays) // workdays number between dates

Notice that all functions can miss weekends (Saturday and Sunday), as well as holidays if they are stated. See the WORKDAY for more consistency in deciding which days are considered weekends. NETWORKDAYS as well as the INTL function.

7. WEEKDAY & WEEKNUM

The WEEKDAY function in Excel may be used to determine the day of the week from a date. WEEKDAY returns a number ranging from 1 to 7, indicating Sunday, Monday, Tuesday, and so forth. To find the week number in a given year, use the WEEKNUM function.

D5			fx	=WEEKDAY(B5)			
	A	B	C	D	E	F	G
1							
2		*Figuring out the week # and day-of-week*					
3							
4		Date		WEEKDAY	WEEKNUM		
5		Sun, 11-Nov-2018	-->	1	46		
6		Mon, 12-Nov-2018	-->	2	46		
7		Tue, 1-Jan-2019	-->	3	1		
8		Fri, 1-Feb-2019	-->	6	5		

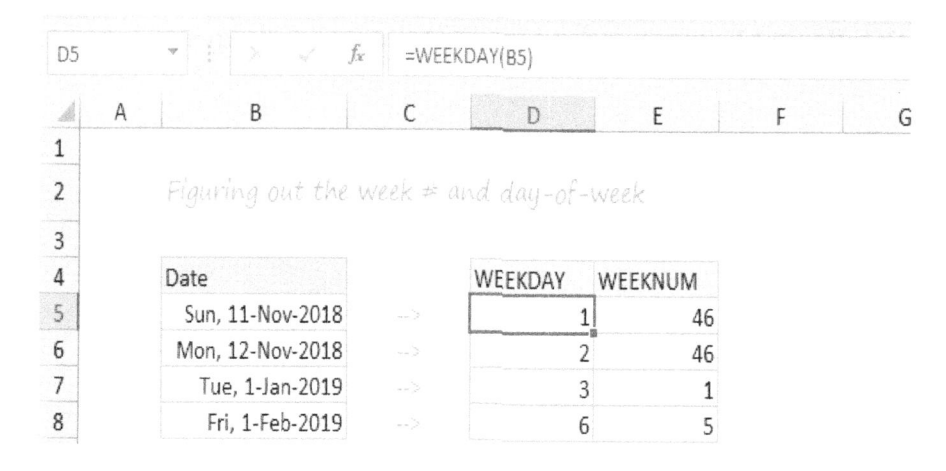

=**WEEKDAY** (date) // returns number 1 to 7

=**WEEKNUM** (date) // returns week number in year

5.2 Information Functions

1. ISBLANK
2. ISERROR
3. ISNUMBER
4. ISFORMULA

These functions are explained below step by step

1. ISBLANK

Syntax	= ISNUMBER (value)
Return value	A logical value (TRUE or FALSE)
Arguments	Value - Checking the value

78

Purpose	Check for a numerical value.

When a cell contains an integer, the Excel ISNUMBER function returns TRUE; otherwise, it returns FALSE. ISNUMBER may be used to verify that a cell includes a numeric value or that a function's output is a number.

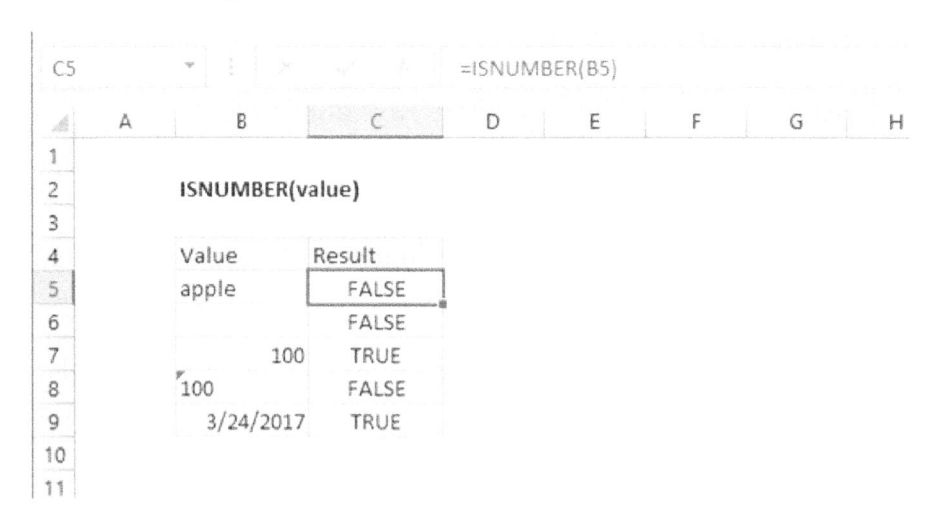

	A	B	C	D
2		ISNUMBER(value)		
4		Value	Result	
5		apple	FALSE	
6			FALSE	
7		100	TRUE	
8		100	FALSE	
9		3/24/2017	TRUE	

C5 = =ISNUMBER(B5)

To see whether a value is a number, use the ISNUMBER function. When the value is numeric, ISNUMBER returns TRUE; otherwise, it returns FALSE.

If A1 includes a number or a formula that returns a numeric value, for example, =ISNUMBER (A1) would return TRUE. ISNUMBER will return FALSE if A1 contains the text.

Notes

- Value is usually supplied as a cell reference, but you can evaluate the outcome by wrapping various functions and formulas within ISNUMBER.

- Since Excel dates and times are numeric, ISNUMBER would return TRUE for them and FALSE for numbers inserted as text.

- ISNUMBER is one of the IS functions, which are a set of functions.

2. ISERROR

Syntax	= ISERROR (value)
Return value	A logical value (TRUE or FALSE)
Arguments	The meaning that will be checked for any errors.
Purpose	Checking the value

The ISERROR function in Excel returns TRUE for every error type, including #N/A, #REF!, #VALUE!, #DIV/0!, #NAME?, #NUM! And #NULL! When you use ISERROR with the IF function, you can check for errors and show a custom message or perform a different calculation if one is detected.

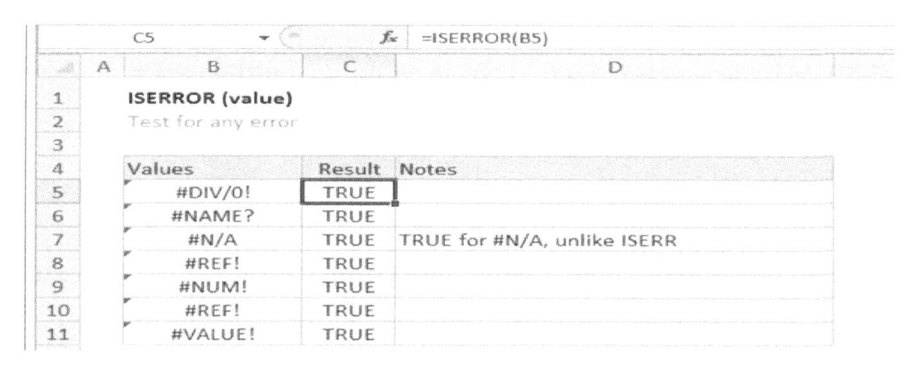

	A	B	C	D
1		ISERROR (value)		
2		Test for any error		
3				
4		Values	Result	Notes
5		#DIV/0!	TRUE	
6		#NAME?	TRUE	
7		#N/A	TRUE	TRUE for #N/A, unlike ISERR
8		#REF!	TRUE	
9		#NUM!	TRUE	
10		#REF!	TRUE	
11		#VALUE!	TRUE	

C5 ▾ fx =ISERROR(B5)

Notes

- To see whether a cell contains some error messages, such as #N/A, #VALUE!, #REF!, #DIV/0!, #NUM!, #NAME?, or #NULL!, use the ISERROR function.

- =ISERROR(A1), for example, will return TRUE if A1 is showing one of the errors listed above and FALSE otherwise.

- Value is usually provided as a cell address, but it may also be used to catch errors in more complicated formulas.

3. ISNUMBER

Syntax	= ISNUMBER (value)
Return value	A logical value (TRUE or FALSE)
Arguments	The value to examine.
Purpose	Check for a numerical value.

When a cell contains a number, the Excel ISNUMBER function returns TRUE; otherwise, it returns FALSE. ISNUMBER may be used to verify that a cell includes a numeric value or that a function's output is a number.

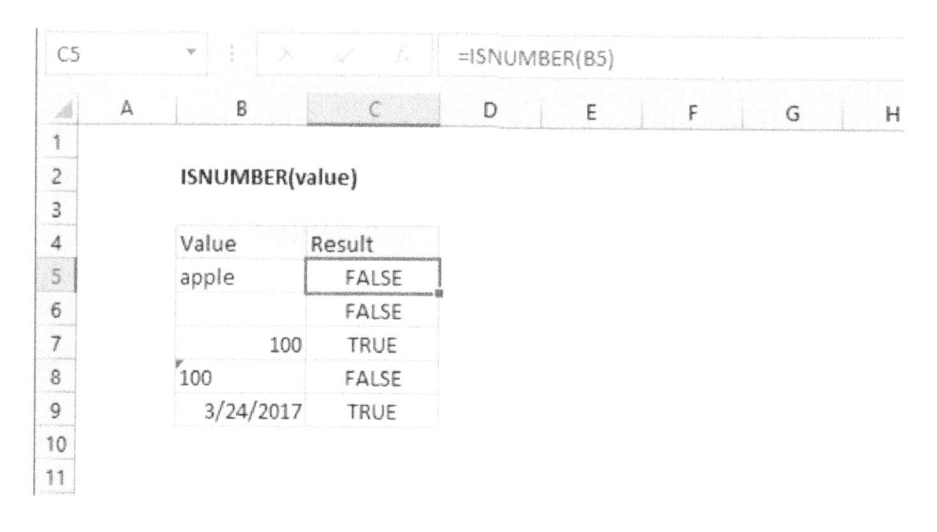

	A	B	C	D	E	F	G	H
1								
2		ISNUMBER(value)						
3								
4		Value	Result					
5		apple	FALSE					
6			FALSE					
7		100	TRUE					
8		'100	FALSE					
9		3/24/2017	TRUE					
10								
11								

To see whether a value is a number, use the ISNUMBER function. When the value is numeric, ISNUMBER returns TRUE; otherwise, it returns FALSE.

If A1 includes a number or formula that returns a numeric value, for example, =ISNUMBER(A1) would return TRUE. ISNUMBER will return FALSE if A1 includes text.

Notes

- Value is usually supplied as a cell address, and you can evaluate the outcome by wrapping other functions and formulas within ISNUMBER.

- Since Excel dates and times are numeric, ISNUMBER would return TRUE for them and FALSE for numbers typed as text.

- ISNUMBER is one of the IS functions, which are a set of functions.

4. ISFORMULA

Syntax	= ISFORMULA (reference)
Return value	TRUE or FALSE
Arguments	reference - reference to a cell or a range of cells
Purpose	Check to see if a cell has a formula.

The ISFORMULA method in Excel returns TRUE if a cell includes a formula and FALSE otherwise. ISFORMULA returns TRUE when a cell includes a formula, irrespective of the formula's error OR output conditions.

	A	B	C	D	E
1		ISFORMULA (reference)			
2					
3		Month	Total	Is formula?	Formula
4		January	$100.00	FALSE	#N/A
5		February	$125.00	TRUE	=C4+(C4*25%)
6		March	$156.25	TRUE	=C5+(C5*25%)
7		April	$195.31	TRUE	=C6+(C6*25%)

D4 : fx =ISFORMULA(C4)

The ISFORMULA function can be used to check whether a cell includes a formula. If a cell includes a formula, ISFORMULA returns TRUE; otherwise, it returns FALSE.

You should use a keyboard shortcut to briefly highlight all calculations in a worksheet.

Use the FORMULATEXT function to extract and present a formula.

Notes

- In Excel 2013, the ISFORMULA function was added.

5.3 Logical Functions

Many advanced formulas depend on Excel's logical functions as a platform. The conditional values TRUE or FALSE are returned by logical functions.

1. AND Function
2. OR Function
3. NOT Function
4. IFERROR Function
5. IFNA Function
6. IF Function
7. IFS Function

1. AND Function

Syntax	= AND (logical 1, [logical 2], ...)
Return value	TRUE if all premises evaluate TRUE; if not, FALSE
Arguments	Logical 1 - The 1st condition or logical value to examine. Logical 2 - The 2nd condition or logical value to examine.
Purpose	Evaluate multiple conditions with AND

The AND feature in Excel is a logical function that is used to require several conditions at the same time. AND either returns TRUE or FALSE. Using =AND(A1>0, A1<10) to see whether a number in A1 is higher than 0 and less than ten. The AND feature, which can be paired with OR function, can be used as a logical test within the IF function to eliminate additional nested IFs.

	A	B	C	D	E	F	G
			C5		fx	=AND(B5>75,B5<90)	
1		AND function					
2		Return TRUE if all conditions are TRUE					
3							
4		Score	>75 AND <90				
5		76	TRUE				
6		81	TRUE				
7		78	TRUE				
8		90	FALSE				
9		85	TRUE				
10		100	FALSE				

The AND function can be used to evaluate several logical conditions at once, approximately 255 in all. Every logical condition (logical 1, logical 2, & so on) must either return FALSE or TRUE or arrays, references containing logical values.

The AND function evaluates all input values and returns TRUE only if all of them are TRUE. The AND feature will return FALSE if every value evaluates too FALSE.

Notes

- The AND function doesn't really sensitive.
- Wildcards are not supported by the AND function.
- Arguments of text values or void cells are overlooked.
- If no logical values are identified or generated during evaluation, the AND function will return #VALUE.

2. OR Function

Syntax	OR (logical 1, [logical 2], ...)
Return value	If all of the arguments' test to TRUE, TRUE; otherwise, FALSE.
Arguments	Logical 1 - The 1st condition or logical value to examine. Logical 2 - The 2nd condition or logical value to examine. (Optional)

Purpose	Evaluate multiple conditions with OR

The function OR is a logical function that can be used to evaluate several conditions at once. OR returns one of two values: FALSE or TRUE. To measure A1 for x or y, for example. OR function, which can be merged with the AND function, can be used as a logical measure within the IF function to prevent additional nested IFs.

You may use the OR feature to measure several conditions at once, approximately 255 in all. Each logical state (logical1, logical2, and so on) must either return FALSE OR TRUE or be sequences or references containing logical values.

OR function will test all of the input values & return TRUE if all of them are TRUE. OR function would return FALSE if all logical evaluate FALSE.

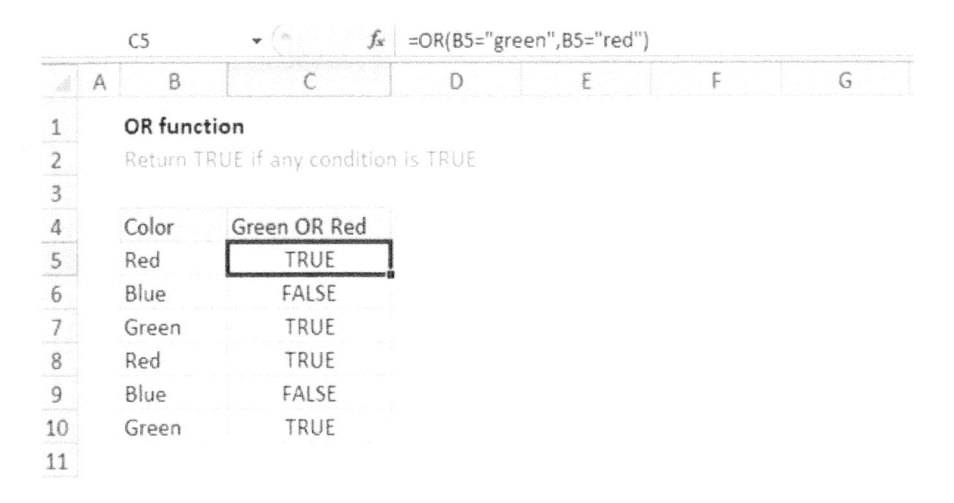

	A	B	C	D	E	F	G
			C5		f_x =OR(B5="green",B5="red")		
1		OR function					
2		Return TRUE if any condition is TRUE					
3							
4		Color	Green OR Red				
5		Red	TRUE				
6		Blue	FALSE				
7		Green	TRUE				
8		Red	TRUE				
9		Blue	FALSE				
10		Green	TRUE				
11							

Notes

- Each logical condition must return TRUE or FALSE or be sequences or references of logical values.

- Arguments of text values or void cells are overlooked.

- When no logical values are detected, the OR feature will return #VALUE.

3. NOT Function

Syntax	=NOT (logical)
Return value	Reversed logical value
Arguments	Logical - Logical expression or value that may either be TRUE or FALSE when evaluated.
Purpose	Reverse results or arguments

The NOT function in Excel returns the inverse of a logical or boolean attribute. NOT returns FALSE when granted TRUE. NOT returns TRUE when granted FALSE. To reverse a logical value, use the NOT element.

```
D6        fx  =NOT(ISBLANK(B6))
    A     B           C           D         E    F    G    H
1
2         NOT(logical)
3         Reverse a logical or boolean result value
4
5         Value       ISBLANK     NOT(ISBLANK)
6         65          TRUE        TRUE
7         59          FALSE       TRUE
8         75          TRUE        TRUE
9
10
```

Notes

To reverse logical argument or a value, use the NOT function:

- NOT returns TRUE when logical is FALSE.

- NOT returns FALSE when logical is TRUE.

4. IFERROR Function

Syntax	= IFERROR (value , value if error)
Return value	For error conditions, you can specify a value.
Arguments	Value - To search for an error, enter a value, a relation, or a formula. Value if error - When an error is found, this is the value to return.
Purpose	Detected and handle errors

When a formula detects an error, the Excel IFERROR feature returns a custom outcome, and when no error is found, it returns a normal result. IFERROR is a simple way to catch and handle errors without the need for nested IF statements.

	A	B	C	D	E	F
1						
2		IFERROR(value, value_if_error)				
3		Trap error and display a more friendly result				
4						
5		Sales	Units	Average price	Comments	
6		300	62	4.84		
7		14	0	0.00	< Would display #DIV/0	
8		200	11	18.18		
9		120	7	17.14		
10		634	80	7.93		
11						

D7 = IFERROR(B7/C7,0)

When an error is found in a calculation, the IFERROR feature "catches" it and returns an alternate result or formula.

To catch and treat errors caused by other formulas or operations, use the IFERROR feature. #N/A, #REF!, #VALUE!, #NUM!, #DIV/0!, #NAME?, or #NULL! are all errors that IFERROR looks for.

Notes

- Where a value is left blank, it is seen as a null string ("") rather than a mistake.

- When the value if error parameter is set to an empty string (""), no error message is shown.

- When IFERROR is used as an array rule, it returns an array of values, one for each value cell.

- The IFNA feature in Excel 2013+ can be used to directly trap and manage #N/A errors.

5. **IFNA Function**

Syntax	= IFNA (value, value_if_na)
Return value	For #N/A mistakes, the value provided.
Arguments	Value - To verify for an error, used the value, reference, or formula. Value if na - If a #N/A error is detected, this is the value to return.
Purpose	Detected and handle #N/A errors

When a formula produces a #N/A error, the Excel IFNA feature returns a custom result, and when no error is found, it returns a normal result. IFNA is a clever way to capture and treat #N/A errors when ignoring any other errors.

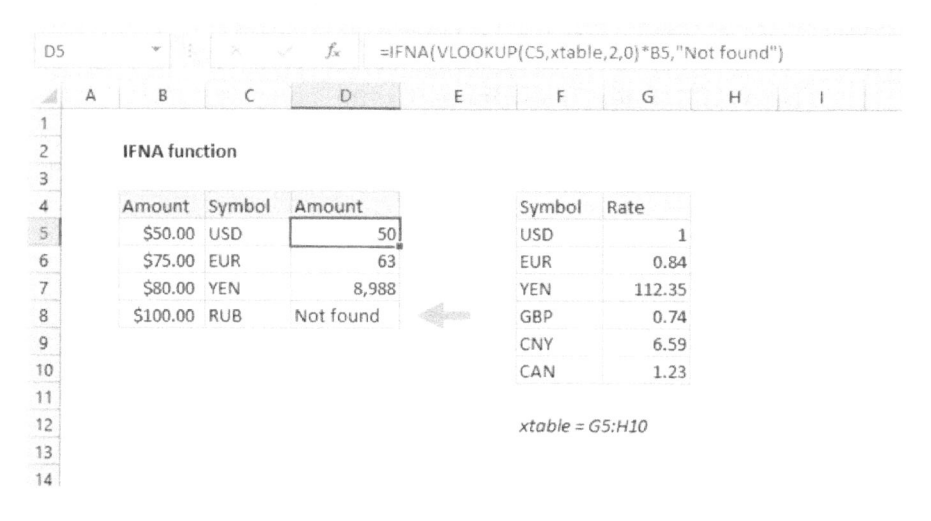

	A	B	C	D	E	F	G	H	I
1									
2		IFNA function							
3									
4		Amount	Symbol	Amount			Symbol	Rate	
5		$50.00	USD	50			USD	1	
6		$75.00	EUR	63			EUR	0.84	
7		$80.00	YEN	8,988			YEN	112.35	
8		$100.00	RUB	Not found			GBP	0.74	
9							CNY	6.59	
10							CAN	1.23	
11									
12							xtable = G5:H10		

Formula in D5: `=IFNA(VLOOKUP(C5,xtable,2,0)*B5,"Not found")`

Use the IFNA function to catch and treat #N/A errors in formulas, particularly those that use MATCH, VLOOKUP, HLOOKUP, and other lookup functions. The IFNA function only handles #N/A errors, so any other errors that a formula can produce will still be shown.

You may also capture #N/A errors with the IFERROR function, but IFERROR would also catch other errors.

Notes

- Where a value is left empty, it is seen as a null string ("") rather than a mistake.

- When the value_if_na parameter is set to an empty string (""), no error message is shown.

6. IF Function

Syntax	= IFNA (value, value_if_na)
Return value	For #N/A mistakes, the value provided.
Arguments	Value - To verify for an error, used the value, reference, or formula. Value if na - If a #N/A error is detected, this is the value to return.
Purpose	Detected and handle #N/A errors

IF function executes a logical test & returns one result if the outcome is TRUE & another if the result is FALSE. =IF(A1>70,"Pass","Fail"), for example, to "pass" scores over 70. IF functions may be nested to measure several conditions. To expand the logical evaluation, the IF function may be coupled with logical features like AND and OR.

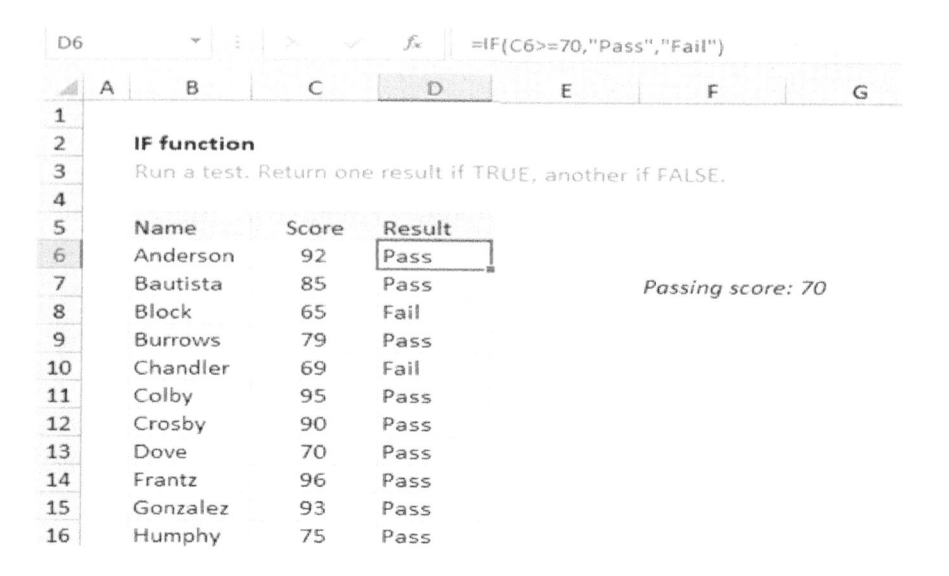

	A	B	C	D	E	F	G
1							
2		IF function					
3		Run a test. Return one result if TRUE, another if FALSE.					
4							
5		Name	Score	Result			
6		Anderson	92	Pass			
7		Bautista	85	Pass		Passing score: 70	
8		Block	65	Fail			
9		Burrows	79	Pass			
10		Chandler	69	Fail			
11		Colby	95	Pass			
12		Crosby	90	Pass			
13		Dove	70	Pass			
14		Frantz	96	Pass			
15		Gonzalez	93	Pass			
16		Humphy	75	Pass			

D6: `=IF(C6>=70,"Pass","Fail")`

The IF function can be utilised to perform a logical test and reacts in a particular way based on whether the answer is TRUE or FALSE. The first statement, logical test, is a phrase that returns TRUE or FALSE when evaluated. While both values if true and value if false are optional, at least one must be given. IF will return a value, a cell connection, or another formula as a consequence.

Notes

- Use the COUNTIF or COUNTIFS functions to conditionally count things.

- Use the SUMIF or SUMIFS functions to conditionally sum things.

- If all of the IF function's arguments are arrays, the IF function evaluates each element of the array.

7. IFS Function

Syntax	=IFS (test 1, val 1, [test 2, val 2], ...)
Return value	The value corresponds to the first TRUE outcome.
Arguments	Test 1 – 1st logical test. Value 1 - Result when test 1 TRUE. Test 2, value 2 - Second value/ test pair [optional]
Purpose	Test several conditions & return the first one that is true.

The Excel IFS method runs multiple experiments and returns the first TRUE outcome as a value. To test different conditions without several nested IF statements, use IFS function. IFS allows formulas to be simpler and quicker to learn.

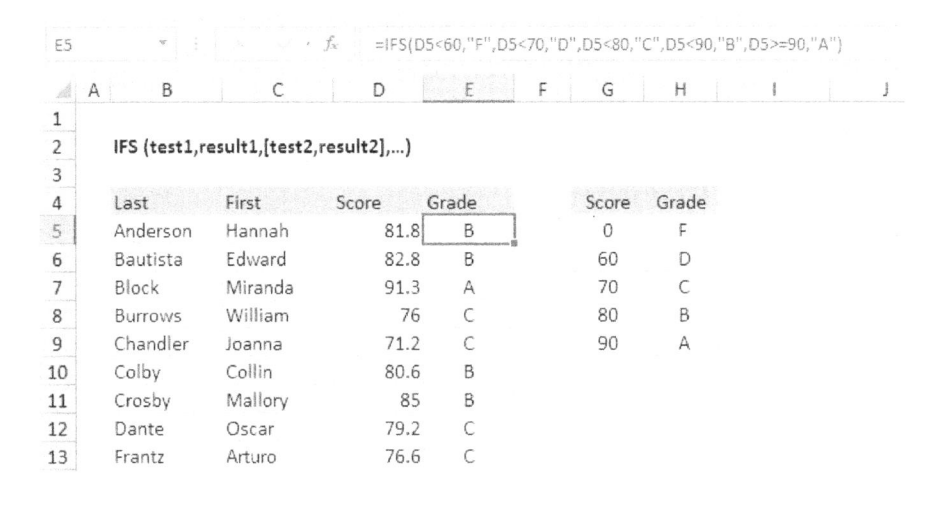

E5				fx	=IFS(D5<60,"F",D5<70,"D",D5<80,"C",D5<90,"B",D5>=90,"A")				
	A	B	C	D	E	F	G	H	I	J
1										
2		IFS (test1,result1,[test2,result2],...)								
3										
4		Last	First	Score	Grade		Score	Grade		
5		Anderson	Hannah	81.8	B		0	F		
6		Bautista	Edward	82.8	B		60	D		
7		Block	Miranda	91.3	A		70	C		
8		Burrows	William	76	C		80	B		
9		Chandler	Joanna	71.2	C		90	A		
10		Colby	Collin	80.6	B					
11		Crosby	Mallory	85	B					
12		Dante	Oscar	79.2	C					
13		Frantz	Arturo	76.6	C					

Notes

- If all parameters are FALSE, the IFS feature does not have a built-in default value to use.

- Enter TRUE as a final test & value to return if/when no other conditions are met to have a default value.

- The results in all logical evaluations must be TRUE or FALSE. Every other outcome would result in a #VALUE! Error from IFS.

- IFS can return the #N/A error unless no logical tests return TRUE.

5.4 Lookup & Reference Functions

1. VLOOKUP Function
2. HLOOKUP Function
3. MATCH Function
4. HYPERLINK Function
5. GETPIVOTDATA Function
6. OFFSET Function

These functions are explained below step by step

1. VLOOKUP Function

Syntax	=VLOOKUP (value, table, col index, [range lookup])
Return value	From a table, the matched value.
Arguments	value - value to search for in the table's first column. Table - Table on which a value can be retrieved. Col index - The table column from which a value is to be retrieved. Range lookup TRUE = approx. match. FALSE = identical match.
Purpose	Match on the first column to look up a value in a table.

VLOOKUP is an Excel feature that allows you to lookup data in a vertically ordered table. VLOOKUP allows for approximate & exact matching, as well as partial matches using wildcards (*?). The first column of the table transferred to VLOOKUP must include the lookup values.

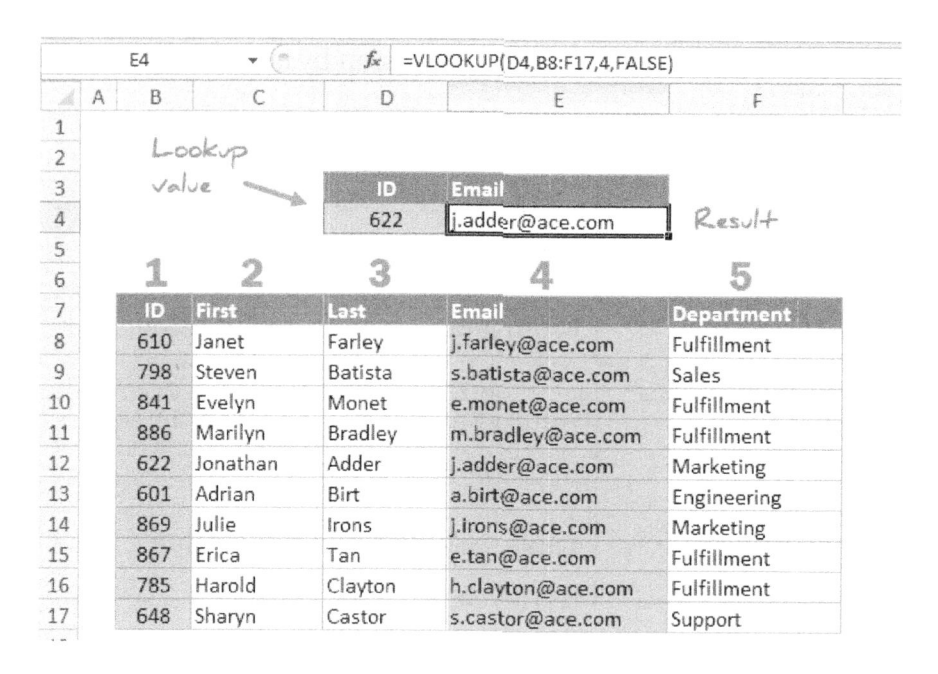

	A	B	C	D	E	F
				fx	=VLOOKUP(D4,B8:F17,4,FALSE)	
1						
2		Lookup				
3		value		ID	Email	
4			→	622	j.adder@ace.com	Result
5						
6		1	2	3	4	5
7		ID	First	Last	Email	Department
8		610	Janet	Farley	j.farley@ace.com	Fulfillment
9		798	Steven	Batista	s.batista@ace.com	Sales
10		841	Evelyn	Monet	e.monet@ace.com	Fulfillment
11		886	Marilyn	Bradley	m.bradley@ace.com	Fulfillment
12		622	Jonathan	Adder	j.adder@ace.com	Marketing
13		601	Adrian	Birt	a.birt@ace.com	Engineering
14		869	Julie	Irons	j.irons@ace.com	Marketing
15		867	Erica	Tan	e.tan@ace.com	Fulfillment
16		785	Harold	Clayton	h.clayton@ace.com	Fulfillment
17		648	Sharyn	Castor	s.castor@ace.com	Support

The letter V stands for vertical

VLOOKUP is used to retrieve data from a table that looks like this:

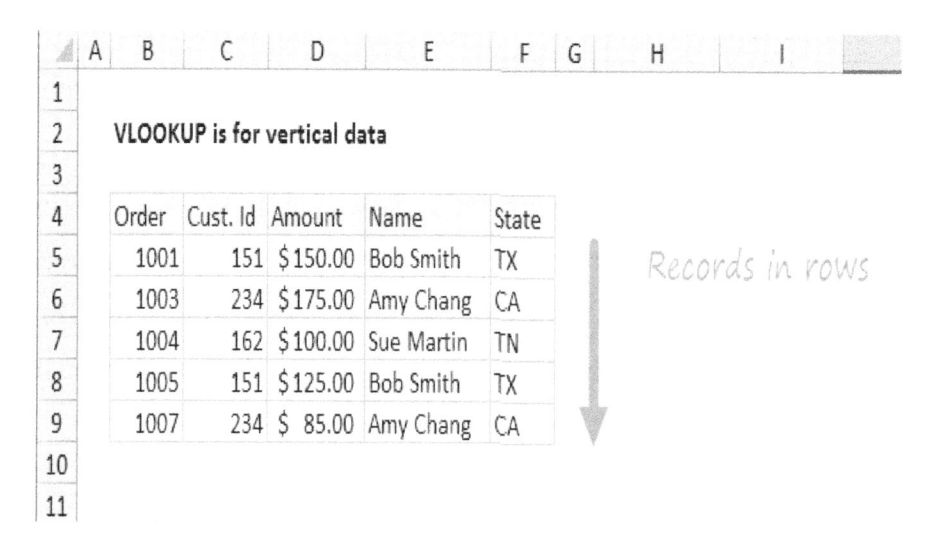

	A	B	C	D	E	F	G	H	I
1									
2		VLOOKUP is for vertical data							
3									
4		Order	Cust. Id	Amount	Name	State			
5		1001	151	$150.00	Bob Smith	TX		Records in rows	
6		1003	234	$175.00	Amy Chang	CA			
7		1004	162	$100.00	Sue Martin	TN			
8		1005	151	$125.00	Bob Smith	TX			
9		1007	234	$ 85.00	Amy Chang	CA			
10									
11									

VLOOKUP will get the Cust. ID, Amount, Name, & State for any order by using the Order number in column B as a lookup value. For an instant, the formula to get the customer details for order 1004 is:

= VLOOKUP (1004, B5:F9,4, FALSE) // returns "Sue Martin"

VLOOKUP is a lookup function that is built on column numbers

Imagine that any column in the table is counted from left to right by using VLOOKUP. Provide the required amount as the "column index" to get a value from a certain column. The column index for retrieving the first name, for example, is 2:

	A	B	C	D	E	F	G	H	I
1									
2		1	2	3	4				
3		ID	First	Last	Email		ID	622	
4		610	Janet	Farley	j.farley@ace.com		First	Jonathan	2
5		798	Steven	Batista	s.batista@ace.com		Last	Adder	3
6		841	Evelyn	Monet	e.monet@ace.com		Email	j.adder@ace.com	4
7		886	Marilyn	Bradley	m.bradley@ace.com				
8		622	Jonathan	Adder	j.adder@ace.com				
9		601	Adrian	Birt	a.birt@ace.com				
10		869	Julie	Irons	j.irons@ace.com				
11		867	Erica	Tan	e.tan@ace.com				
12		785	Harold	Clayton	h.clayton@ace.com				
13		648	Sharyn	Castor	s.castor@ace.com				
14									

H4 fx =VLOOKUP(H3,B4:E13,2,FALSE)

Columns 3 & 4 should be used to retrieve the last name & email address:

VLOOKUP only appears to be right

VLOOKUP will only look in one direction: yeah. The information you're looking for (result values) can be found in every column to the right of the lookup values:

	A	B	C	D	E	F	G
1							
2		First	Last	ID	Email	Department	
3		Janet	Farley	610	j.farley@ace.com	Fulfillment	
4		Evelyn	Monet	841	e.monet@ace.com	Fulfillment	
5		Marilyn	Bradley	886	m.bradley@ace.com	Fulfillment	
6		Jonathan	Adder	622	j.adder@ace.com	Marketing	
7		Julie	Irons	869	j.irons@ace.com	Marketing	
8		Erica	Tan	867	e.tan@ace.com	Fulfillment	
9		Harold	Clayton	785	h.clayton@ace.com	Fulfillment	

If we want to use VLOOKUP with ID, we can only lookup Email and Department

Other Comment

- Range lookup determines whether or not a value would fit exactly. The default value is TRUE, which means that non-exact matches are permitted.

- Set range lookup to FALSE if an exact match is required and TRUE if a non-exact match is required.

- A non-exact match would trigger the VLOOKUP feature to match the closest value in the table, which is still less than the value if range lookup is TRUE (the default setting).

- The VLOOKUP function would allow a non-exact match if range lookup is omitted, but it would use an exact match when one exists.

- If range lookup is TRUE (the default), ensure that the first row of the table's lookup values are ordered in ascending order. Otherwise, VLOOKUP could return an unexpected or incorrect result.

- The values in very first column of the table don't want to be sorted if range lookup is FALSE (require exact match).

2. HLOOKUP Function

Syntax	=HLOOKUP (value, table, row index, [range lookup])
Return value	From a table, the matched value.
Arguments	value - Value to look up. Table - Table on which the data can be retrieved. Row index - Number of the rows to extract data from.

	Range lookup - A boolean value that indicates whether the match is exact or approximate. True – Default = approximate match.
Purpose	Match the first row of a table to find a value.

HLOOKUP is an Excel feature that allows you to look up and extract information from a particular table row. The "H" in HLOOKUP stands for "horizontal," indicating that lookup values start in the table's first row and move horizontally to the right. HLOOKUP allows for approximate and precise matching, as well as incomplete matches using wildcards (*?).

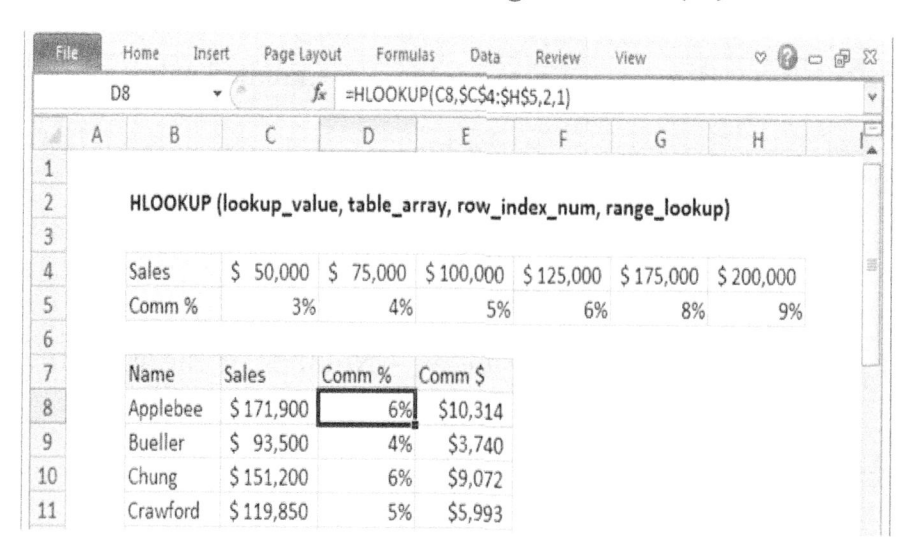

	A	B	C	D	E	F	G	H
1								
2		HLOOKUP (lookup_value, table_array, row_index_num, range_lookup)						
3								
4		Sales	$ 50,000	$ 75,000	$ 100,000	$ 125,000	$ 175,000	$ 200,000
5		Comm %	3%	4%	5%	6%	8%	9%
6								
7		Name	Sales	Comm %	Comm $			
8		Applebee	$ 171,900	6%	$10,314			
9		Bueller	$ 93,500	4%	$3,740			
10		Chung	$ 151,200	6%	$9,072			
11		Crawford	$ 119,850	5%	$5,993			

D8: =HLOOKUP(C8,$C$4:$H$5,2,1)

Notes on use

HLOOKUP scans first row of a table for a value. It retrieves a value from the given row in the match column. When the lookup values are in the 1st row of a table, use HLOOKUP. When the lookup values are in the 1st column of a table, use VLOOKUP.

- Range lookup determines whether or not a value would fit exactly. The default value is TRUE, which means that non-exact matches are permitted.

- To require an exact match, set range lookup to FALSE.

- A non-exact match would trigger the HLOOKUP feature to match the closest value inside the table, which is still less than the value if the range lookup is TRUE (the default setting).

- The HLOOKUP feature would allow a non-exact match if range lookup is omitted, but it would use an accurate match if one exists.

- If range lookup is TRUE (the default), ensure that the first row of the table's lookup values are ordered in ascending order. Otherwise, HLOOKUP could return an unwanted or incorrect result.

- The values in the first row of the table don't want to be sorted if range lookup is FALSE (require exact match).

3. MATCH Function

Syntax	=MATCH (lookup value, lookup array, [match type])
Return value	A number that represents a lookup array position.
Arguments	lookup value - Value in lookup array to match. Lookup array - An array reference or a set of cells. Match-type - 1 indicates the same or next smallest value, 0 indicates the exact match, and -1 indicates the same or next largest value.
Purpose	Match the first row of a table to find a value.

MATCH is an Excel feature that locates a lookup value's location in a row, column, or table. MATCH facilitates both estimated and precise matching, as well as incomplete matches using wildcards (*?). MATCH is often used in combination with the INDEX function to extract a value from a matched location.

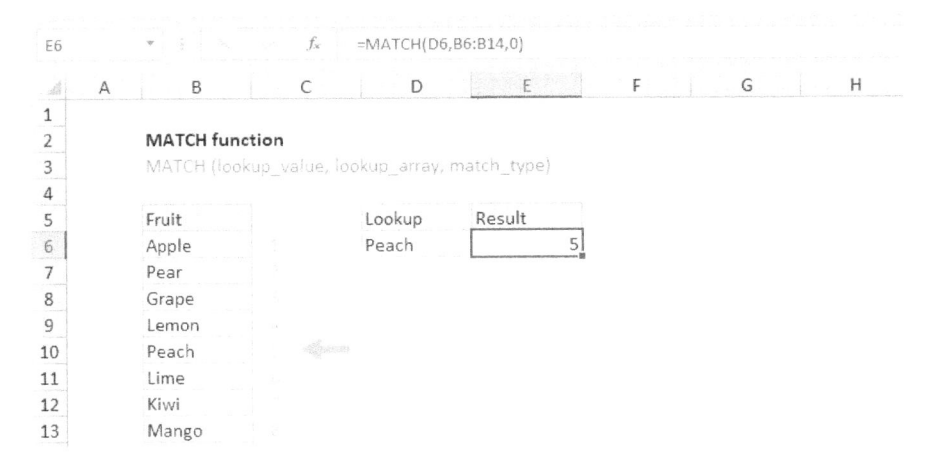

	A	B	C	D	E	F	G	H
1								
2		MATCH function						
3		MATCH (lookup_value, lookup_array, match_type)						
4								
5		Fruit		Lookup	Result			
6		Apple		Peach	5			
7		Pear						
8		Grape						
9		Lemon						
10		Peach						
11		Lime						
12		Kiwi						
13		Mango						

Cell E6 formula: =MATCH(D6,B6:B14,0)

Notes on use

- The MATCH feature is used to find a value's location in a set or array. The formula in cell E6 in the screenshot above, for example, is set to get the direction of the value throughout cell D6. Since the lookup value (peach) is in 5th place in the range B6:B14, the MATCH function returns 5.

= MATCH (D6, B6 : B 14, 0) // returns 5

- The MATCH feature will conduct exact and estimated matches, as well as partial matches, using wildcards (*?). As mentioned below, there are three different match types (set by the match type argument).

- In order to collect a value at a specific (matched) location, the MATCH feature is often paired with the INDEX function. To put it another way, MATCH determines the spot, while INDEX returns the value at that place.

Details on the match type

The form of the match is optional. If no match form is defined, 1 is used by default (exact or next smallest). It's often referred to as an approximate match where the match type is 1 or -1. Keep in mind, as seen in the table below, MATCH can find an accurate match with both match types:

Match type	Behaviour	Details
1	Approximate	MATCH looks for the most significant attribute that is smaller than or equal to the lookup value. Sorting the lookup array in ascending order is needed.

0	Exact	MATCH looks for the first value that matches the lookup value. There is no need to sort the lookup array.
-1	Approximate	The smallest value larger than or equal to the lookup value is found by MATCH. Sorting the lookup array in descending order is needed.
	Approximate	If match form isn't specified, it defaults to 1 and behaves as described above.

Caution

If you'd like an exact match, make sure to set match form to zero (0). MATCH's default setting of 1 will lead to findings that "appear normal" but are actually incorrect. Providing meaning for match type explicitly serves as a strong reminder of desired actions.

4. HYPERLINK Function

Syntax	= HYPERLINK (link location, [friendly name])
Return value	clickable hyperlink
Arguments	Link location - The route to the file or page to be opened. Friendly name - The text that will appear in a cell as a hyperlink.
Purpose	Create a clickable link.

The HYPERLINK feature in Excel creates a hyperlink from a specified destination with a "friendly name." To create a clickable hyperlink with a formula, use the HYPERLINK function. The HYPERLINK feature will create connections to workbook places, internet sites, and network server archives.

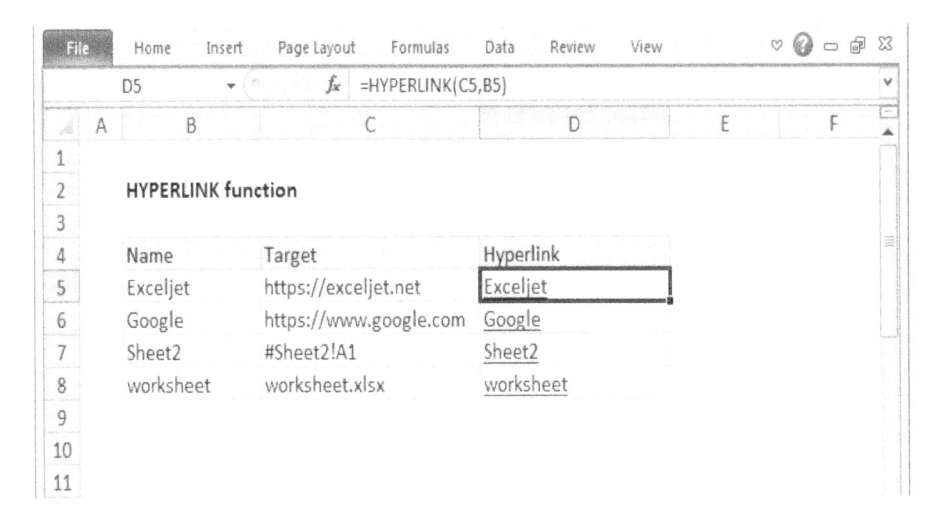

	A	B	C	D	E	F
1						
2		HYPERLINK function				
3						
4		Name	Target	Hyperlink		
5		Exceljet	https://exceljet.net	Exceljet		
6		Google	https://www.google.com	Google		
7		Sheet2	#Sheet2!A1	Sheet2		
8		worksheet	worksheet.xlsx	worksheet		

Cell D5: =HYPERLINK(C5,B5)

Build connections to workbook sites, internet websites, or network service files using the HYPERLINK function.

Excel will open the file or page identified by link location whenever a user clicks a cell that contains the HYPERLINK feature. A cell connection or called range, a path to a file on a local drive, a path to a file on a server using (UNC) the Universal Naming Convention, or a web route in (URL) Uniform Resource Locator format are all valid options for Link location.

Notes

- Link location should be defined as a text string enclosed in quotation marks or as a cell relation containing the text connection path.

- If friendly name is not specified, the link location will be shown as the friendly name.

- Using the arrow keys to pick a cell that includes HYPERLINK without moving to the destination. Alternatively, keep down the mouse button when clicking on the cell before the cursor shifts.

5. **GETPIVOTDATA Function**

Syntax	=GETPIVOTDATA (data field, pivot table, [field1, item1], ...)
Return value	Data requested
Arguments	Link location - The route to the file or page to be opened. Friendly name - The text that will appear in a cell as a hyperlink.
Purpose	In a formula, get data from a pivot table.

Instead of using cell references, the GETPIVOTDATA feature in Excel will query a pivot table and extract relevant data depending on the pivot table layout.

To query an internal pivot table and extract relevant details depending on the pivot table configuration, use the GETPIVOTDATA feature. The very first argument (data field) specifies the value field that will be queried. The second point (pivot table) is a pointer to every cell in a pivot table that already exists.

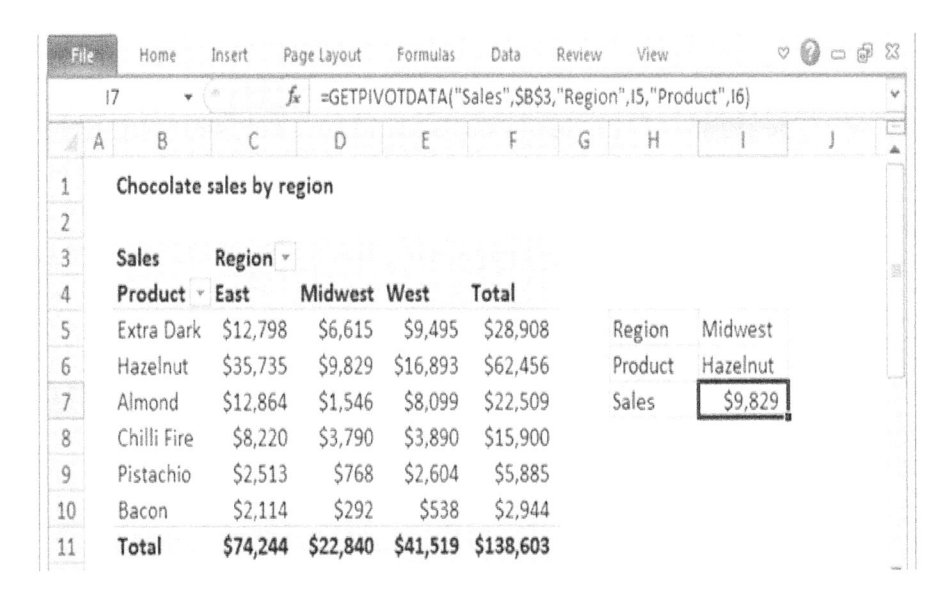

	A	B	C	D	E	F	G	H	I
1		Chocolate sales by region							
2									
3		Sales	Region						
4		Product	East	Midwest	West	Total			
5		Extra Dark	$12,798	$6,615	$9,495	$28,908		Region	Midwest
6		Hazelnut	$35,735	$9,829	$16,893	$62,456		Product	Hazelnut
7		Almond	$12,864	$1,546	$8,099	$22,509		Sales	$9,829
8		Chilli Fire	$8,220	$3,790	$3,890	$15,900			
9		Pistachio	$2,513	$768	$2,604	$5,885			
10		Bacon	$2,114	$292	$538	$2,944			
11		Total	$74,244	$22,840	$41,519	$138,603			

Formula bar: `=GETPIVOTDATA("Sales",$B$3,"Region",I5,"Product",I6)`

Additional arguments are given in the form of field/item pairs that serve as filters to restrict the data retrieved depending on the pivot table's layout. To restrict sales data to sales in the East area, you might use the field "Region" with the object "East."

This instructs the GETPIVOTABLE feature to retrieve data from the pivot table's sector "Sales," which starts in cell B3. For the commodity "Hazelnut," the data is restricted to the "Midwest" area. Cells I5 and I6 have the values for Region and Product.

When you link a value cell in a pivot table, the GETPIVOTABLE feature is automatically created. To stop this, quickly type the cell's address into the address bar (instead of clicking). Disable "Generate GETPIVOTABLE" in the Pivot TableTools > Options > Options menu if you want to completely disable this function (far left, below the name of the pivot table).

Notes

- The name of the data field should be enclosed in double-quotes, as must the field/item values.

- If some fields are misspelt, GETPIVOTDATA will display a #REF error.

6. OFFSET Function

Return value	cell reference
Arguments	Reference - The starting point, which may be specified as a cell reference or a set. Rows - Number of rows below starting reference to offset. Cols - Number of the columns to offset from starting reference to the right. Height - The returned reference's height in rows. Width - The returned reference's width in columns.
Purpose	Create the reference offset based on the given starting point.

The OFFSET feature in Excel returns a reference to a range created with five inputs:

- a starting point
- a row offset
- a column offset
- a row height, and
- a column width.

In formulas that include a complex spectrum, OFFSET comes in handy.

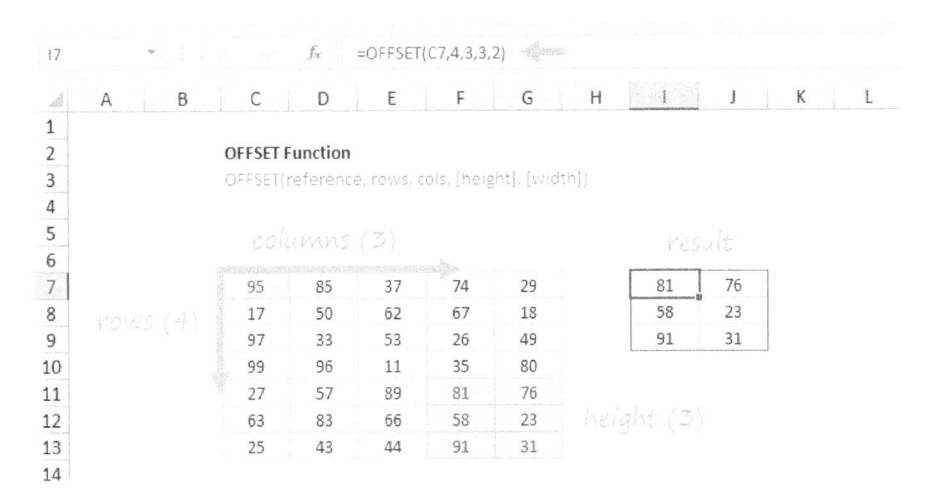

	A	B	C	D	E	F	G	H	I	J	K	L
1												
2			OFFSET Function									
3			OFFSET(reference, rows, cols, [height], [width])									
4												
5			*columns (3)*						*result*			
6												
7			95	85	37	74	29		81	76		
8		*rows (4)*	17	50	62	67	18		58	23		
9			97	33	53	26	49		91	31		
10			99	96	11	35	80					
11			27	57	89	81	76					
12			63	83	66	58	23		*height (3)*			
13			25	43	44	91	31					
14												

Formula bar: =OFFSET(C7,4,3,3,2)

One cell or a number of cells may be used as the preliminary step (the comparison argument). The number of cells to **offset** from starting point is defined by the rows & cols arguments. The volume of the range generated is determined by the height & width claims, which are optional. When height & width are left blank, the height & width of comparison are used instead.

OFFSET's key function is to enable formulas to adapt dynamically to accessible data or user feedback. To ensure the source data is still up to date, the OFFSET feature may be used to provide a complex named selection for charts/pivot tables.

Chapter 6: Shortcut Keys in Excel

This session is solely for the purpose of grasping the concept of some unusual ns and other functions. This chapter is broken into two sections: the first introduces you to keyboard shortcut keys, and the second explains the office components that are related to Excel. You will be able to perform the following tasks after completing this session:

- Using the shortcut keys on the keyboard.
- Excel components that have been installed.

As we discussed in Word, shortcut keys are always the most efficient method. The shortcut implies that you should be able to finish the task in the shortest amount of time and effort possible. While it is recommended to follow the menu and mouse instructions to the letter, it is highly encouraged to complete the task using the shortcut keys to save time and improve productivity. The following subjects linked to shortcut keys are discussed below; please read them, and we are confident that you will find the best solution and boost your working speed by at least 30% in your normal curriculum. The key combination is solely for teaching you which key combination works in which mode to finish the task.

Key Combination

1. Keys for moving and scrolling in a worksheet or workbook.
2. Keys for previewing and printing a document.

3. Keys for working with worksheets, charts, and macros.

6.1 Moving and scrolling in a worksheet or workbook

Key Sequence Required	Function
Arrow keys	One cell can be moved up, down, left, or right.
CTRL+arrow key	Go to the very edge of the current data area.
HOME	Return to the start of the row.
CTRL+HOME	Return to the start of the worksheet.
CTRL+END	Move to the last cell on the worksheet, which is normally A1 and is located at the intersection of the rightmost used column and the bottom-most used row (in the lower-right corner).
PAGE DOWN	Go one screen down.
PAGE UP	Increase the size of the screen.
ALT+PAGE DOWN	Right-click and drag one screen to the right.

ALT+PAGE UP	Shift to the left one screen.
CLTRL+PAGE DOWN	Return to the workbook's next sheet.
CLTRL+PAGE UP	Return to the previous workbook sheet.
CTRL+F6 OR CTRL+TAB	Go to the next window or workbook
CTRL+SHIFT+F6 or CTRL+SHIFT+TAB	Return to the previous window or workbook.
SHIFT+F6	In a workbook where SHORTCUT KEYS IN EXCEL has been separated, go to the previous pane.
CTRL+BACKSPACE	To see the active cell, scroll down.
F5	The Go-To dialogue box will appear.
SHIFT+F5	Show the Last Dialog Box
SHIFT+F4	Rep the previous Find action (same as Find Next)

TAB	On a protected worksheet, move between unlocked cells.
F6	In a workbook that has been split, go to the next page.

6.2 Keys for previewing and printing a document

Key Sequence Required	Function
CTRL+P or CTRL+SHIFT+F12	The Print dialogue box will appear.
Arrow Keys	Move around the page when zoomed in.
PAGE UP or DOWN	Move by one page when zoomed out.
CTRL+UP ARROW or CTRL+LEFT ARROW	Move to the first page when zoomed out
CTRL+DOWN ARROW or CTRL+RIGHT ARROW	Move to the last page when zoomed out

6.3 Key for working with worksheets, charts, and macros

Key Sequence Required	Function
CTRL+F11 or ALT+SHIFT+F1	Add a new worksheet.
F11 or ALT+F1	Make a chart with the current range.
ALT+F8	The Macro dialogue box will appear.
ALT+F11	The Visual Basic Editor will appear.
CTRL+F11	Create a macro sheet in Microsoft Excel 4.0.
CTRL+PAGE DOWN	Move to the sheet in the workbook.
CTRL+PAGE UP	Return to the previous workbook sheet.
SHIFT+CTRL+PAGE DOWN	In the workbook, select the current and next sheet.
SHIFT+CTRL+PAGE UP	In the workbook, select the current and previous sheets.

ENTER	Move down in the selection by completing a cell entry.
ALT+ENTER	In the same cell, start a new line.
CTRL+ENTER	Fill the current entry into the given cell range.
SHIFT+ENTER	Move up in the selection by completing a cell entry.
TAB	Move to the right in the selection after completing a cell entry.
SHIFT+TAB	Complete a cell entry and move to the left in the selection.
ESC	Cancel a cell entry
BACKSPACE	Delete the character to the left of the insertion point or the selection altogether.
DELETE	Delete the character to the right of the insertion point. or delete the selection
CTRL+DELETE	Delete text to the end of the line
Arrow Keys	One character can be moved up, down, left, or right.
HOME	Return to the start of the line.

F4 or CTRL+Y	Repeat the previous action.
SHIFT+F2	Edit a comment in a cell
CTRL+SHIFT+3	Row and column tables can be used to generate names.
CLTRL+D	Fill in the gaps.
CTRL+R	Fill in the blanks to the right.
CTRL+3	Define a name.

6.4 Keys for use with Pivot Table and PivotChart reports.

Layout keys for PivotTable and PivotChart reports:

- To activate the menu bar, press F10.

- To access the Pivot Table toolbar, use CTRL+TAB or CTRL+SHIFT+TAB.

- To select the menu to the left or right, or to switch between the main menu and a submenu, press the LEFT ARROW or RIGHT ARROW keys.

- To select the area, you want to move the selected field, press ENTER (on a field button) and the DOWN ARROW and UP ARROW keys.

6.5 First and Fast Tip

In a worksheet or workbook, keys for moving and scrolling are provided. Press ALT+SPACEBAR and then X to expand the Help window to fill the screen. Press ALT+SPACEBAR, then R to return the window to its previous size and location.

- Scrolling in a worksheet or workbook is controlled by a set of keys.

- Keys to move around a worksheet with End mode turned on Keys to go around a worksheet with SCROLL LOCK turned on.

Conclusion

The updated Excel models have all you need to get started and become a professional, as well as a wide range of valuable features. To save you time, MS Excel identifies trends and organizes results. Create spreadsheets quickly and conveniently from models or from scratch, then use modern features to conduct calculations.

It includes both basic and advanced software that can be used in almost any business environment. The Excel database helps you to build, access, update, and exchange data with others quickly and easily. You can generate spreadsheets, data tables, data logs, budgets, and more by reading and updating excel files attached to emails. When you gain a better understanding of various definitions, you'll be able to recognize the new tools and features that Excel offers its users. The reality is that Excel functionality can accommodate almost any individual or business necessity. What you need to do is put in the effort to broaden your skills. The learning curve for developing your skills may be steep, but with practice and time, you will notice that things become second nature. After all, a guy improves by repetition.

Mastering these basic Excel skills is what you need to do to make your life easier—and maybe impress those in your workplace. However, remember that no matter how familiar you are with this helpful instrument, there is still something fresh to learn. Whatever you do, keep developing your Excel skills—it will not only help you keep track of your own earnings, but it can also lead to a better potential job opportunity.

To conclude, wisdom is often said to be strong, and there's no easier way to motivate yourself than by honing your talents and the worth of your business with expertise and technology.

Thank you and Good Luck!